ORGANIC ARCHITECTURE | THE OTHER MODERNISM

ORGANIC ARCHITECTURE | THE OTHER MODERNISM

PHOTOGRAPHS BY **ALAN WEINTRAUB**

TEXT BY **ALAN HESS**

Gibbs Smith, Publisher
Salt Lake City

For Uncle Red
— A. W.

For Bruce and Ranji Mendle
— A. H.

First Edition
10 09 08 07 06   5 4 3 2 1

Photographs © 2006 Alan Weintraub
Text © 2006 Alan Hess

Published by
Gibbs Smith, Publisher
PO Box 667
Layton, Utah 84041

Orders: 1.800.748.5439
www.gibbs-smith.com

Library of Congress Cataloging-in-Publication Data

Hess, Alan.
   Organic architecture : the other modernism /
Alan Hess ; photographs by
Alan Weintraub. — 1st ed.
      p. cm.
   Includes bibliographical references.
   ISBN 1-58685-857-2
   1. Organic architecture—United States. 2.
Architecture, Domestic—United
States. 3. Architecture—United States—20th
century. I. Weintraub, Alan.
II. Title.

NA7208.H468 2006
728'.37—dc22

2006010131

Designed by Zand Gee
Printed and bound in Hong Kong

Front Jacket: Desert house, Ken Kellogg, 2004
Back Jacket: Sun Valley house, Bart Prince, 1992
Page 2: Sun Valley house, Bart Prince, 1992
Page 4: Crescent house, Wallace Cunningham, 2004
Page 7: Bowler house, Lloyd Wright, 1963
Pages 10–11: Fireplace detail, Purcell-Cutts house,
   Purcell and Elmslie, 1913
Page 276: Window detail, Desert house,
   Ken Kellogg, 2004

CONTENTS

6 Introduction

12 Chapter 1: 1900–1920

38 Chapter 2: 1920–1940

76 Chapter 3: 1940–1990

186 Chapter 4: 1990–Present

272 Acknowledgments

273 Bibliography

273 Reference List

274 Index

CHAPTER 1
1900–1920

16 **Frank Lloyd Wright**
Roberts House 1908
River Forest, Illinois

20 **Walter Burley Griffin**
Melson House 1912
Mason City, Iowa

24 **Walter Burley Griffin**
Blythe House 1913
Mason City, Iowa

30 **Purcell and Elmslie**
Purcell-Cutts House 1913
Minneapolis, Minnesota

CHAPTER 2
1920–1940

46 **Frank Lloyd Wright**
Storer House 1923
Los Angeles, California

54 **Lloyd Wright**
Sowden House 1926
Los Angeles, California

64 **Alden Dow**
Hanson House 1934
Midland, Michigan

70 **Paul Schweikher**
Schweikher House 1937
Schaumburg, Illinois

CHAPTER 3
1940–1990

82 **Bruce Goff**
Ford House 1947
Aurora, Illinois

90 **Frank Lloyd Wright**
Mossberg House 1948
South Bend, Indiana

96 **Karl Kamrath**
Kamrath House 1951
Houston, Texas

102 **Sim Bruce Richards**
Richards House 1953
San Diego, California

108 **Bruce Goff**
Pollock-Warriner House 1957
Oklahoma City, Oklahoma

114 **John Lautner**
Silvertop 1959
Los Angeles, California

122 **Eric Lloyd Wright**
Pole House 1960
Los Angeles, California

126 **Charles Haertling**
Willard-Shapiro House 1961
Boulder, Colorado

134 **Lloyd Wright**
Bowler House 1963
Palos Verdes, California

140 **Fay Jones**
Pine Knoll 1964
Little Rock, Arkansas

150 **Fay Jones**
Stoneflower 1965
Eden Isle, Arkansas

156 **Charles Haertling**
Brenton House 1969
Boulder, Colorado

162 **Alfred Browning Parker**
Woodsong 1978
Coconut Grove, Florida

168 **John Lautner**
Segel House 1979
Malibu, California

178 **Aaron Green**
Green House 1993
Philo, California

CHAPTER 4
1990–PRESENT

190 **Mickey Muennig**
Partington Ridge House II 1989
Big Sur, California

206 **Bart Prince**
Sun Valley House 1992
Sun Valley, Idaho

218 **Bart Prince**
Skilken House 1999
Columbus, Ohio

228 **Wallace Cunningham**
Crescent House 2004
San Diego, California

240 **Helena Arahuete**
Roscoe House 2004
Vacaville, California

254 **Ken Kellogg**
Desert House 2004
Joshua Tree, California

INTRODUCTION

"Frank Furness was too good an architect not to know what he was doing and I sometimes think that some of the oddities he introduced were merely the rebellion of a freedom-loving soul who refused to be bound by the rules."

— Albert Kelsey, Furness and Hewitt employee, 1924[1]

A New Style Is Born

In 1873, seventeen-year-old Louis Sullivan passed by the Bloomfield Moore mansion on South Broad Street in Philadelphia. He was not yet the master architect of the Auditorium Building, Wainwright Building, or the National Farmers' Bank, yet the spirit that would create those buildings was already alive in his soul, and this newly constructed building "caught his eye like a flower by the roadside," he later wrote.[2] He was told that the firm of Furness and Hewitt had designed the building. Desiring a career in architecture, Sullivan sought out the architect, Frank Furness, and talked his way into a job. The job lasted less than a year until the Panic of 1873 dried up commissions. Sullivan moved on briefly to the École des Beaux Arts in Paris and then to Chicago and his destiny.

The chord that struck Louis Sullivan when he glimpsed Furness's design has struck many other people in many other places and times. A young Alden Dow visited

Tokyo's Imperial Hotel by Sullivan's master apprentice Frank Lloyd Wright in 1923, and the same passion was ignited. Fourteen years later, Paul Schweikher had the same experience at the same place. Young Fay Jones saw a *Popular Science* newsreel during the Depression that showed another new Wright structure, the Johnson Wax Building, and he was struck by its singular beauty.[3] These buildings embodied a deep and fresh vision of architecture, the landscape, and the machine that made them stand apart.

From such visceral responses to these contemporary yet natural designs, a school of design as well as an enduring premise in American architecture were born. A number of American architects developed a fresh Modern architecture that engaged both contemporary machinery and the ageless natural landscape. It is easiest to call this theme *Organic architecture* because most examples have a common root in the philosophy of Organic design described by Louis Sullivan and Frank Lloyd Wright around 1900. Not all Organic buildings look alike, however. For instance, the intricate geometric plans and ornament of the Purcell and Elmslie firm in the 1910s look nothing like the free-form spaces of John Lautner in the 1960s. What they have in common is the concept of seeing a building's design, structure, use, and life as an organic thing— that is, as a thing that grows from the germ of an idea into a fully articulated, variegated, and unified architectural artifact. In the hands of Bruce Goff or Charles Haertling, these design principles resulted in buildings that literally looked more like living things than traditional architecture. In the hands of Fay Jones or John Lautner, the spatial and visual character of meadows, caves, or forests could be translated into solid architecture. With Walter Burley Griffin or Mickey Muennig, a building was so rooted in its landscape that it seemed to be a part of the geology.

The Scope of Organic Design

It is this book's intention to illuminate the broad brush stroke of Organic residential architecture in America throughout the panorama of twentieth-century Modernism. Organic architecture is a style wide ranging enough to defy easy definition, yet vivid enough for people to know it when they see it. It reached a high point in the mid-twentieth century, but it has roots much deeper in American culture than the European Bauhaus architectural style that combined technology, craftsmanship, and aesthetics. Despite being marginalized at times by the tastemakers and professional magazines, Organic architecture has remained a strong, deep-running current in American culture and design. There are, of course, Organic office buildings (the Price Tower in Bartlesville, Oklahoma, by Wright), coffee shops (Pann's in Los Angeles, California, by Armét and Davis), churches (Sea Ranch Chapel in Sea Ranch, California, by James Hubbell), as well as other building types, but for the sake of clarity and comparison the focus of this book is on residences.

Mid-Century Modern Revival

Today, a renewed interest in the Modern architecture of the mid-twentieth century has led to the coining of the term *Mid-Century Modern*, which is used in shelter magazines, architecture schools, books, and countless product lines for furniture and ornamental fixtures. Yet what passes for Mid-Century Modern today is curiously narrow. The clean, abstract, minimalist lines of the Bauhaus, the International Style, the Case Study Program, and the Joseph Eichler houses fit, but often missing is an entire dimension of design that was actually built and widely popular in the mid-twentieth century: Organic design.

Why Organic architecture has been mostly overlooked in the current Mid-Century

Modern revival can be debated. Perhaps it is because its curves and colors look so starkly different from the Internationalist stylings. Perhaps the neglect reflects the longstanding controversy about what constitutes true Modernism—a debate Frank Lloyd Wright goaded in his design and persona during his lifetime. In any case, this debate continues. The minimalist abstractions of the Case Study houses, which reduce architecture to a chastely edited selection of lines and colors arranged in a stark geometry, reflect a puritan, Apollonian aesthetic perfection. Organic design, however, reflects an exuberant, opulent, and at times extravagant complexity of line, form, texture, structure, and color. Less is not necessarily more in Organic design, and for this it was often sharply attacked by mainstream critics, many of whom controlled the main professional magazines, academies, and publishing houses.

A Brief Review of
Organic Architecture

Organic architects put up a vigorous defense, but the playing field was never equal through the long century. The Prairie style that was based on Organic principles burst on the scene after 1900 and enjoyed two decades of popularity before it faded. Louis Sullivan died at the nadir of his professional reputation and appreciation in 1924 (also, not coincidentally, an all-time low for Organic design). Sullivan was heralded at the time by the likes of Claude Bragdon, an inventive ornamental designer and average architect whose several books are rendered inaccessible as a result of his esoteric Theosophist philosophy. Frank Lloyd Wright was the perfect indefatigable salesman to carry the torch, but he had also hit bottom in the 1920s. Nevertheless, in the late 1930s, Wright reignited the movement. Elizabeth Gordon, a tireless and outspoken editor of *House Beautiful* magazine, also promoted Organic architects in the popular press in the decades after World War II, creating wide awareness. These efforts to promote and spotlight Organic design gained strength from an underlying fact: Organic design has had a long, strong, and ongoing appeal for a large segment of the American public.

As Organic ideas developed in America, prompted by the work of Frank Furness, Louis Sullivan, Frank Lloyd Wright, Bruce Goff, and the rest, its convictions about the interrelation of practical architecture, mystical nature, and progressive technology grew from the intellectual ferment of the new nation, embodied by Ralph Waldo Emerson and Walt Whitman, both of whom Sullivan and Wright admired. Organic architects gave these philosophical ideas tangible form. The walls and floors of Organic structures are often native stone drawn roughly from the earth; the wood and brick are left unpainted, allowing their ingrained textures to create the tone and texture of the surrounding structure.

But the machine is as much a part of Organic architecture as is raw nature. John Lautner used earthen concrete in extraordinary shapes and dimensions because modern technology allowed him to. Bruce Goff used plastics, corrugated metal, and metal guywires next to walls of anthracite coal laid up as masonry. The imagery of Organic designs is as likely to conjure up primordial caves as futuristic spacecraft. The line between indoors and outdoors is often blurred, making the outdoors livable and the indoors a garden.

Of course, similar Organic forms and concepts also evolved outside the United States throughout the century in the expressionist designs of Michel de Klerk and Piet Kramer in Amsterdam, Hugo Häring in Germany, Alvar Aalto and Reima

Pietila in Finland, and Oscar Niemeyer in Brazil. Organic architecture everywhere stands in contrast to the sharply limned Modern ideas of the Bauhaus, where the machine was the dominant image and form giver. The historian ideologues of Modernism painted the triumph of Bauhaus design and its heirs as a historical inevitability. Eschewing the all-too-human temptation to romanticize, this severe, minimalist architecture of, by, and for superhumans was offered as the architectural remedy for the ages. Today we need a reassessment of Organic architecture's role to complement our appreciation of the cool abstractions of Bauhaus Modernism and its legacy. Today's revival of Mid-Century Modern focuses too narrowly on white walls, flat roofs, and vases placed tastefully on large coffee tables. The actual history of the mid-century is much richer than that.

Before this myth that Mid-Century Modernism was limited to minimalism alone spreads farther, it is important to go back and review the actual record of what was built as Modern in the mid-century, when it was a lively movement with disputes and disagreements, villains and heroes, and an active ongoing debate. Fortunately, despite alteration and neglect, a fair cross section of the range of buildings of the last century remains. It is now up to us to seek them out. Organic architecture often took root outside the media centers in places like Midland, Michigan; Norman, Oklahoma; and Fayetteville, Arkansas. And in the present day when computer-aided design helps create the frequently Organic free forms of Rem Koolhaas and Frank Gehry, this book hopes to offer a convenient collection of images of the alternative to Bauhaus Modernism.

To discuss what may have produced Organic architecture in America, we must step back and reconsider a few of the basic assumptions

of the story of American Modern architecture as it has been passed down.

The Development of Organic Architecture

Frank Lloyd Wright (1867–1959) was the North Star of Organic architecture. He worked hard during his ninety-two years to secure his spot in history. He skillfully reinvented the forms expressing his ideas throughout that long career in order to remain a leader—staging dramatic breaks with particular students from time to time to reassert his authority when he felt they were stealing clients or designs.[4]

Organic architecture's reliance on one central figure for its definition and progress had its strategic advantages. Wright is still remembered as America's greatest architect. Yet this fixation on Wright was an odd method for establishing an architectural style. Dozens of good architects were left in his shadow. Organic architecture as a result lacks the institutional breadth of the Bauhaus and its successor International Style, an orchestrated movement intimately tied to academic institutions, large corporate architecture firms in the United States and Europe, and, for many years, leading historians.

Organic architecture took root in America in the West—more specifically, in the Central Plains we now call the Midwest. The de facto capital of the region was Chicago. Though the city was hardly immune to the influence of European taste, its distance from the centers of culture shielded it. The rawness of the enterprise of city building near the frontier—buffered all about by a broad agricultural hinterland, inspired by the raw energy of capitalism, blessed with many talented and inventive architects, freed from many of the conventions and expectations of Boston, New York, or even Philadelphia—

inspired a new architecture. Chicago gave birth in the 1890s to new ideas about commercial buildings (since called the Chicago School) and after 1900 to a suburban residential architecture (since called the Prairie style).

The Prairie School laid the foundation of Organic architecture and swayed the direction of Modernism. It spread from suburban Oak Park throughout the Midwest, producing public buildings, hotels, churches, as well as homes. It rarely found its way to New York or Boston, regions settled in their taste and satisfied with their architecture. It instead found fertile soil in the cities and towns of the Central Plains, in Florida with architect Henry Klutho, in Tucson with the Trost brothers, in San Jose with the work of Wolfe and Wolfe, in Colorado, and in Salt Lake City—in short, in the new, growing regions of the West.

Key Organic Architects

Louis Sullivan (1856–1924) is the great seminal name of Organic architecture; his pithy dictum *form follows function* set up the primacy of structural expression and modern life as the measure of Modern architecture. Two early architects influenced Sullivan. Fellow Bostonian Henry Hobson Richardson (1838–1886) has usually been emphasized in histories of early Modernism. Richardson's clean, understated Romanesque buildings led to the simplicity of Sullivan's first masterpiece, the Auditorium Building. But it was Frank Furness (1839–1912) who gave Sullivan his first job after he left the Massachusetts Institute of Technology. Unapologetically original, Furness boldly mixed modern materials and images into a complete architectural composition.

The impact of Furness's ideas on Sullivan should not be underestimated. It was his bold originality, his daring to think about

buildings in audacious ways, that led to Sullivan's revolution and paved the way for Organic architecture. Furness was controversial in his time and remained so for decades after his death in 1912, after which his reputation declined. Where Richardson's elegant, simplified forms (manifested especially in Chicago's Marshall Field warehouse) fit neatly into a narrative about clean, minimalist Modernism stripping away unnecessary ornament to reveal structural beauty and purity, Furness's muscular buildings were criticized as quirky, awkward, freakish, and ridiculous.[5] He also consciously broke the rules to invent new ones, set the pattern of spirited contrarianism that Frank Lloyd Wright would follow, and grappled with the expression of modern technology in architecture. Philadelphia in the 1870s, after all, was the dynamo of invention and industry in the United States. Furness and his clients had more first-hand experience with the emerging industrial age than the academic or fashionable architects of Boston or New York.

Furness's exaggerated forms embarrassed many historians and critics as they began to write the story of Modernism's heroic birth. But as historian George Thomas has pointed out, Furness also dealt forthrightly with new technological materials, such as iron, and new technological imagery, like trains.[6] That design boldness and inventiveness were highly attractive to the young Louis Sullivan.

There was one other seminal dimension to Furness. His father, William Henry Furness, was a Unitarian minister and friend of Ralph Waldo Emerson. Emerson was often a guest at their home and "played the role of favorite uncle," noted historian George Thomas.[7] Emerson's Transcendentalist philosophy and especially its discussion of Nature inspired Sullivan and Wright. Furness

1   George E. Thomas, Michael J. Lewis, and Jeffrey A. Cohen, *Frank Furness: The Complete Works* (New York: Princeton Architectural Press, 1991), 41.

2   Louis H. Sullivan, *The Autobiography of an Idea* (New York: Dover Publications, 1956), 191.

3   Robert Adams Ivy Jr., *Fay Jones* (New York: McGraw-Hill, 1992), 16.

    "It felt like being thrown two centuries ahead in time," Jones said.

4   Sidney K. Robinson, *The Architecture of Alden B. Dow* (Detroit: Wayne State University Press, 1983), 10.

    For example, Wright broke with Alden Dow in 1949 over his belief that Dow had stolen the Phoenix Civic Center project from him.

5   Thomas, 362.

6   Ibid., 43–49.

7   Ibid., 27.

8   Ibid., 348.

9   Ibid., 27.

10 For an excellent analysis of Furness's blend of technology and nature, of form and function, and of indoors and out, see Thomas, 49.

11 In the early decades of the Modern movement in Europe, architects also explored forms from nature—including crystals, flowers, and trees. The Amsterdam School explored expressionism. Eric Mendelsohn explored free-flowing shapes unlike any others in architectural history. Alvar Aalto used curves in vivid spaces. In Brazil after 1940, Oscar Niemeyer, Eduardo Affonso Reidy, and landscape-architect Roberto Burle Marx also used forms inspired by the lush native landscape of their country. These architects are also a part of the international story of Organic architecture, though not the focus of this book.

got there first, writing in 1878, "In all cases the student must go for knowledge to the fountain-head, Nature."[8] It was after all Emerson himself who brought Furness a stereopticon with scenes of natural landscapes; it is significant that Emerson, the sage philosopher of Organic architecture, used the modern technology of the stereopticon to instruct his young friend in the value of nature.[9] Prefiguring Sullivan's intensely geometric organic ornament, Furness developed an original ornament, part high Victorian, part a riotous hymn to nature—storks with fish in their beaks, frogs, mermaids, and lobsters resided in the woodwork of the high-society dining rooms Furness designed (including the Theodore Roosevelt Sr. home in Manhattan, where young Teddy grew up). Blending modern technology and an appreciation of nature to create original solutions, Furness was the fountainhead of Organic architecture—and a major stream of Modernism.[10]

After his brief but telling contact with Furness, Sullivan moved to Chicago and helped introduce Modern concepts to American architecture. After him, his employee Frank Lloyd Wright carried on the work in spectacular fashion for seventy years, applying Organic ideas to the invention of the Prairie house after 1900 and spawning an entire school. Influenced by Wright, the breakthrough architecture of Mies van der Rohe ("he was the great tree," Mies said of Wright) and Walter Gropius at the Bauhaus won the Modern revolution in Europe just as Wright and his Organic ideas went into a long eclipse after 1920.[11]

Modernism continued during the 1920s, with an infusion of the Art Moderne lines from the Paris Exposition of 1926, the growth of the Bauhaus, the regional modernism of George Fred Keck and others in Chicago, and the work of William

Wurster with his inspiration from the vernacular barns and ranch buildings of Western settlement. The International Style the Europeans developed gained dominance, especially after the political upheaval of the 1930s brought those architects and their ideas spilling over the ocean to Harvard, the Illinois Institute of Technology, and eventually just about every other architecture school and office in the United States.

Against this onslaught, the embers of Organic architecture were kept alive at the hearth of Taliesin, Wright's home in Spring Green, Wisconsin, and in Los Angeles, where two of Wright's colleagues worked with fair success—though mostly out of sight of the mainstream architectural world. One was R. M. Schindler, whose flowing spaces were influenced by Wright. Schindler's use of cave-like concrete structures and open-air gardens in his own house in Los Angeles and the Pueblo Ribera apartments in La Jolla showed an organic character divorced from the architecture of his native Austria. Even more pointedly, Wright's eldest son, Lloyd Wright (born Frank Lloyd Wright Jr.), carried on and embellished his father's ideas.

The surprising resurgence of Wright himself at age sixty-eight in 1935 with the design of Fallingwater produced a host of talented young architects who had either worked with him or who were inspired by his ideas. After a few years working at his side, many moved on to establish their own careers and design predilections in various parts of the United States and the world.

Newly invigorated, the Organic architects added an alternative view of Modernism. During the debates about the course of architecture in the post–World War II era, most architectural schools adopted

International Style theory as their touchstone. Organic architecture had fewer academic champions beyond Wright's Taliesin Fellowship, founded in 1932, and the University of Oklahoma at Norman, where Bruce Goff chaired the School of Architecture from 1947 to 1955. But the growing number and vigor of Organic architects, along with Wright's own entrepreneurial self-promotion, kept Organic architecture in the public eye.

Architects Featured in This Book

The American architects illustrated in this book share similar ideas about architecture and a common American landscape. These facts give their work a cohesive unity worthy of exploration. In the chapters that follow, we present an overview of Organic architecture in America over the last century by showing representative examples by key architects. The selection is not complete; many other talented architects have worked in each period shown. Our intention is to show the evolution of Organic ideas—their variety, their variations, and their detours. Above all, we hope to reveal an architecture that has demonstrated an extraordinary longevity and adaptability in American culture. It taps a deep current in American thought, imagery, and desire. •

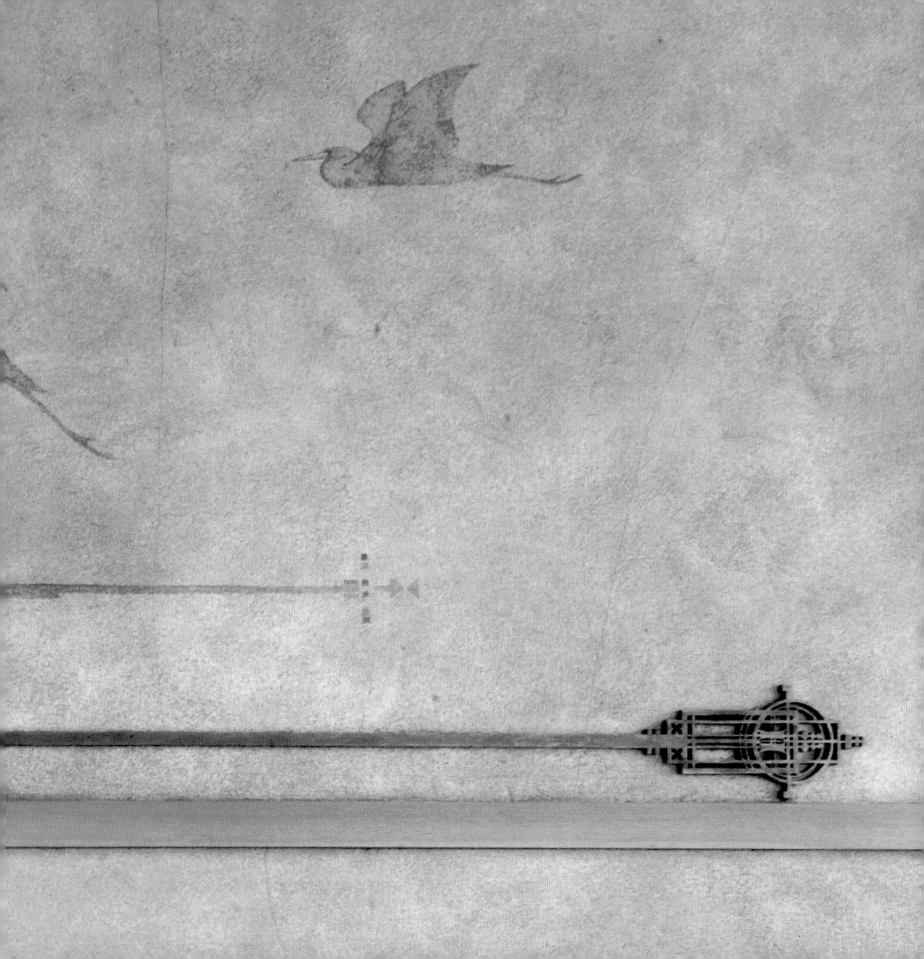

CHAPTER 1900–1920

Chicago as Architectural Laboratory

Modern architecture was still young in 1900. Chicago in the late nineteenth century was one of the central laboratories for architects shaping buildings to the new ways people lived and the new materials at hand. People saw and felt the Modern era's effects in innovations, such as central heating, mechanical mass transportation, factories, and materials like cast iron. Even after being destroyed by fire in 1871, Chicago had only grown in size, influence, and prosperity. Its pragmatic, raucous, and rawly capitalist citizens did not care about precedent and fashion as much as people in New York, Boston, or even Philadelphia. Chicago's atmosphere was the one which encouraged young architects like Louis Sullivan to invent. By the 1890s, the Chicago skyscrapers had startled the world.

As the modern metropolis of Chicago reached up, it also reached out. The elevated commuter trains only recently running back and forth from suburban edge to downtown center were as essential to the new city as Otis's reliable new elevators in the skyscrapers. The suburbs, initially conceived at Tuxedo Park, New York, as enclaves for the wealthy, became accessible to the middle class as well. Now it was possible for the middle class to work downtown and live amid nature in quiet suburbia on the fringe of the city.

Prairie Style—the Origin of Organic Architecture

Modern residential architects found a new clientele for themselves in suburbs like Oak Park, Evanston, Riverside, and Lake Forest. The result was the Prairie style, a fully formulated Modern architecture rooted in the American Midwest and its progressive political and intellectual landscape at a time before Europe had found its modern architectural rhythms. The idea of nature as well as omnipresent technology pervaded Chicago's architectural explorations. The philosophical influence of Ralph Waldo Emerson blended with the design concept of an organic integration of elements and the tangible suburban setting of trees, lawns, rivers, and parks.

Of these modern architects, we know today primarily of Frank Lloyd Wright, but in 1900 he was only one of many talented and daring young architects carving out a career and competing for clients. Wright referred to a "prairie school" in 1936, but at the time it was just a group of young, similarly minded designers.[1] The style that we today call Prairie was part of an exploratory push by architects to use new materials to create an original, marketable, and popular new residential style. It would be a startling contrast to the Victorian and period revival homes that constituted the majority of homes of the day. Wright, the master rhetorician of the movement, called those exteriors "be-deviled—that is to say, mixed to puzzle-pieces, with corner-boards, panel-boards, window-frames, corner-blocks, plinth-blocks, rosettes, fantails, ingenious and jigger work in general."[2]

Wright and his fraternity were only a segment of the Chicago architecture profession, but they were a true community. Many of these like-minded architects—including Robert Spencer, Richard Schmidt,

Hugh Garden, Dwight Perkins, Howard Van Doren Shaw, Myron Hunt, James Gamble Rogers, and Wright—had adjoining offices in Steinway Hall downtown. They often met for lunch to converse, belonged to the same clubs and associations, and showed their latest work in the same exhibits. Other architects, like George Maher and employees of large firms, joined in the search for a new style and contributed to it. Adler and Sullivan's office employed creative young architects, including William Gray Purcell and George Elmslie. Wright, however, was fired in 1893 for moonlighting. Later, Wright's own office would attract talented designers, including Walter Burley Griffin, Barry Byrnes, William Drummond, and Marion Mahony. Louis Sullivan, who had left the partnership with Adler in 1895, was their grand master, the older and revered architect who inspired emulation.

This group of architects designed churches, warehouses, schools, and shops, as well as houses in Chicago and throughout the Midwest. Not all favored a new style. James Gamble Rogers tended toward Gothic; Howard Van Doren Shaw had a prosperous career serving wealthy clients who had once been his college mates from Yale; and the rich did not on the whole favor any revolutionary new style. In the press of actual business, the development of a conceptual architecture was a luxury but one that a number of architects in this group took seriously. Many were captivated by the ideas of the contemporary Arts and Crafts movement born in England. But whereas William Morris and Elbert Hubbard were leery of the machine and its effects, the Prairie architects fully embraced the machine and all its manifestations as a welcome tool and inspiration. "The engine, the motor, and the battle-ship [are] the works of art of the century," Wright wrote.[3] Even though this early Organic architecture,

which originated with the Prairie style, idealized a life surrounded by the verdant landscape of River Forest or Oak Park—and years later by the wilder settings of the eastern Pennsylvania forest or the Arizona desert—it did not encourage a reversion to primitive living. This capability was quintessentially Modern.

The Prairie architects introduced the basic ideas of Organic architecture as it would unfold through the century. The Prairie houses sought to break down the line between the house and its natural site: roof lines often emphasized the broad prairie horizon; long stretches of windows purposefully framed views; and the walls evaporated, at least as far as the technology of the time allowed. Inside, rooms interlocked to create new spaces that flowed together to create a larger organic unity, eliminating the boxy rooms of traditional architecture. Built-in furnishings united structure and daily functions. Modern heating, lighting, and plumbing were essential. Over the whole inside and out, ornament grew out of the rhythms of the structure and spaces, with unified lines emphasized by long, simple strips of woodwork. Intricate, colorful art-glass windows formed bands of light along the walls. Natural forms of leaves, vines, and flowers often formed the basis of this ornament; Louis Sullivan's inventive ornament joining natural forms and complex geometries had set a formidable standard.

The Prairie architects also pioneered the use of many materials—especially new ones— that later Organic architects would incorporate. Walter Burley Griffin's Blythe house in Iowa used poured-in-place concrete (as had Frank Lloyd Wright's 1906 Unity Temple) to create a massive and foursquare structure. Later in his career, Griffin developed a system of concrete-block construction called the Knitlock

system in Australia in 1917; that was prior to the textile-block system that Frank Lloyd Wright and Lloyd Wright developed with great effect in Los Angeles around 1920.[4] Concrete in its many forms became a favorite organic material frequently used by Wright's apprentices Alden Dow in the 1930s and John Lautner in the 1950s.

The Prairie architects' use of concrete exemplified their design ethos. Though solid and rocklike in final form, concrete could be molded into virtually any shape, such as discrete blocks to be piled one atop the other or a monolithic form that provided the structure of an entire house. Architects used concrete's inherent plastic character as the starting point for their design, and they expressed that character in their design. Concrete-block houses became crystalline forms; poured-in-place houses became stunning singular shapes. Brazilian Oscar Niemeyer, another mid-century architect who appreciated the characteristics of concrete, praised "the versatile spirit of the reinforced concrete . . . [which] required something different as architecture made up of dreams and fantasy, of curves and enormous free spaces, of extraordinary spans."[5]

Prairie houses were made out of wood from trees and brick from the earth's mud, but Prairie architects' interest in Organic ideas went even deeper than the use of natural materials. Architects spoke of organic as a concept—of building designs evolving in an integrated manner from the function, site, structure, and materials; this was a revolutionary contrast to the orderly conventions of the architectural establishment's Classical and Beaux-Arts designs.

As the Prairie architects worked in this new manner of invention, the Organic design philosophy evolved. They threw out precedent and sought new principles to derive form. Frank Lloyd Wright summed up this approach in the 1910 preface to the Wasmuth portfolio of his works: "In Organic Architecture, then, it is quite impossible to consider the building as one thing, its furnishings another and its setting and environment still another. The Spirit in which these buildings are conceived see all these together at work as one thing. All are to be studiously foreseen and provided for in the nature of the structure. All these should become mere details of the character and completeness of the structure."[6]

The principles of Organic design were pointedly at odds with the mainstream architecture. In the new Organic style, one architectural element related to another in an organic, unified manner. Its forms or ornament might specifically echo the natural forms of trees, flowers, or geology. The building blended with its site. Frank Lloyd Wright wrote in 1910, "Education, world-wide, is to be blamed for not inculcating in students the conception of Architecture as an organic expression of the Nature of an actual building-problem in place and time; teaching them not to look to this actual Nature for the elements of its development in accord with principles easily found in Nature and seen in nature-organisms."[7] From the beginning, Organic architecture set up in opposition to the establishment.

In the 1890s, the exact form of the new architecture was still undetermined as many architects explored many avenues. Wright himself was a restless talent. The vertical Heller house contrasted with the exaggerated horizontal lines of the Robie house; the blocky, foursquare Heurtley house was quite unlike the interwoven solids and voids of the Gale house. Other progressive architects in turn-of-the-century

Chicago likewise brought their own interpretations to the Prairie style. Most colleagues of Wright, both in his office and out, had architectural training (unlike Wright) and were from his generation.[8] One of the most prominent of this group was Walter Burley Griffin, who was only nine years younger than Wright.

WALTER BURLEY GRIFFIN

A native of Oak Park, Walter Burley Griffin (1876–1937) attended the University of Illinois architectural department, graduating in 1899. He set up offices at Steinway Hall along with the other progressive architects, and two years later joined Wright's office in Oak Park, where he worked alongside his future wife Marion Mahony (a talented architect, graduate of the Massachusetts Institute of Technology, and superb renderer), William Drummond, Barry Byrne, and others. Griffin continued at the Oak Park studio for four years before opening his own office.

Griffin had quickly mastered the vocabulary of the Prairie style. His designs skillfully composed one- and two-story wings, with porte cocheres or porches integrated to emphasize horizontal lines. Brick foundation walls were articulated to create a strong foundation to tie the house to the ground. Griffin had his own interests in form and interior spaces, including tall peaked roofs and emphatic fascia lines. Inside he used the Prairie style of plain surfaces of brick-framing fireplaces, with wood trim contrasting with light-toned plaster walls, to create detail and ornamental counterpoint.

Griffin also explored other original ideas. In the 1912 J. G. Melson house in Mason City, Iowa, he created a strong statement of Organic architecture distinct from anything Wright had done at the time. Underscoring the competition between Prairie architects,

Melson had asked Wright to design a house for the same site, but he chose Griffin as the architect for the house that was built. Rugged and masculine, the structure seems to emerge from the steep limestone bluff overlooking Willow Creek. This was Organic architecture that used its natural setting as inspiration for form, material, and texture.

Mason City, the site of a hotel and bank designed by Wright as well as several houses by various Prairie School architects, illustrated the Midwestern ease with the new progressive style. The Melson house is part of Rock Crest–Rock Glen, an eighteen-acre subdivision planned by Griffin that winds along and overlooks a river and parkland. The house's great corner piers are clad in rough, irregular stone masonry that seems to grow out of the site's stone rubble. The design blends confidently with the earth, expressing the ambiguous line between natural setting and human structure, sealing the embrace of nature and civilization. The house's crystalline lines, drawn from the geology, offer a nontraditional, ahistoric source of form and ornament. The tactile textures and fanciful, exaggerated ornamental keystones above the windows prefigure the bold, unconventional elements that Bruce Goff would use in the future.

James E. Blythe, a partner in the Rock Crest development, commissioned several houses for the tract, including his own 1913 house by Griffin. Unlike the Melson house, the upper walls were smooth plaster rising from calmer limestone ashlar foundation and terrace walls. The rocklike massiveness expressed Griffin's selection of reinforced concrete for the structure. Wright apprentice John Lautner would perfect the expressive potential of poured-in-place concrete fifty years later with a daring thinness and free-form composition at which

Griffin's experiments only hinted. The contained, symmetrical forms of these Griffin houses illustrated one of the directions taken by Organic design principles in the early years. There was not, and there would not be in years to come, a single expression for Organic ideas.[9]

PURCELL and ELMSLIE

William Gray Purcell (1880–1965), like Walter Burley Griffin, was an Oak Park native who was well aware of his neighbor Wright's houses. He studied architecture at Cornell University, graduating in 1903, and worked briefly for Louis Sullivan at the recommendation of his future partner George Elmslie (1871–1952). Scottish-born Elmslie moved to the United States in 1884 and trained in architecture in the office of J. L. Silsbee, Wright's first employer in Chicago. In 1889, Elmslie moved to Sullivan's office at Wright's recommendation, where he stayed two decades before partnering with Purcell.

After working for other progressive architects in Los Angeles and San Francisco, Purcell returned to Chicago in 1906 and then traveled in Europe, meeting the Dutch architect Henrik Berlage. Clearly Purcell was pursuing modern ideas, and in 1909 he entered into partnership with Elmslie, the year Wright left his wife and family for Europe with his mistress Mamah Cheney. Though Purcell did not work for Wright, the two men were acquaintances, and Purcell discussed specific designs with Wright. During their partnership, Purcell and Elmslie became one of the most successful Prairie-style architectural firms, designing homes, churches, banks, and public buildings throughout the Midwest. A series of small-town bank buildings in the upper Midwest took root alongside Sullivan's to establish the Prairie style as a firm public architecture of the small towns and prosperous agricultural regions of the Midwest.

Though firm and graceful exponents of the Prairie style, Purcell and Elmslie's wide-ranging work allowed them to experiment with new types and forms that Wright did not. The 1913 William and Edna Purcell house in Minneapolis shows Purcell and Elmslie's originality and mastery of the Prairie style. The wide eaves, bands of art-glass windows, and strong geometry are clearly Prairie style, yet the composition and the interior are unlike Wright's. The house is small and linear on an in-town lot, but the architects varied the interior space with split levels. Ingeniously, the dining room, which was raised a half story, overlooks the sunken living room, effectively creating the unified flowing spaces of Organic design with the intimacy of comfortable spaces.

The Spread of the Prairie Style

The Prairie style spread throughout North America in the work of Wolfe and Wolfe in Northern California; Bugenhagen and Turnbull in Saskatoon, Saskatchewan; Henry Klutho in Florida; Antonin Neckendorn in San Juan, Puerto Rico; and Henry C. Trost in Tucson, Arizona. The movement was so widely spread and its creativity so unconventional that it took years, even decades, for most critics to grasp the salient features of the style. Their eyes had been trained in Classical design, and the Prairie style looked harsh and odd. Wright's majestic Coonley house, today considered a Prairie School masterpiece, was called a "freak" by one critic in 1911.[10] Another critic in *American Architect and Building News* in 1902 said of the structure:

One is ashamed of the trivial spirit that is abroad here among us. There is a set of younger men here in Chicago who foster all this sort of thing. They have among them men with artistic spirit and feeling but their aim seems to be always to strive for the semi-grotesque, the

1 H. Allen Brooks, *The Prairie School* (New York: W. W. Norton & Co., Inc., 1972), 13.

2 Edgar Kaufmann and Ben Raeburn, eds., *Frank Lloyd Wright: Writings and Buildings* (Cleveland, OH: The World Publishing Co., 1960), 40.

3 Brooks, 20.

4 Ibid., 6.

5 Joseph Maria Botey and Miquel Dalmau, *Oscar Niemeyer* (Barcelona: Fundacao Caixa, 1990), 249–50.

6 Kaufmann, 102.

7 Ibid., 99.

8 Brooks, 72.

Griffin's 1903 William Emery house shows the close relationships among architects and clients interested in the new architecture. Both Wright and Griffin were personal friends of the Emerys, and Wright had designed other structures in the neighborhood. Griffin was selected over Wright because he seemed more flexible in meeting the Emerys' ideas while creating a house with progressive ideas. The practical struggle for common clients would continue to interweave through the history of Organic architecture.

9 Brooks, 255.

Early drawings show that Griffin drew on Mayan architecture as a source in composing and ornamenting the house. Wright later incorporated similar themes in the 1915 German warehouse and the concrete block houses of Los Angeles.

10 Ibid., 198.

11 Ibid., 45.

12 Ibid., 294.

13 Ibid., 87.

catchy. Their compositions lack the best principles of honest design. Their aim seems to be to impress upon the beholder the belief that they are so filled with artistic inspirations and ideas that the flood cannot be held back for a minute, but must be dashed down onto paper as fast as ink or lead can carry it.[11]

Self-indulgent, eye-catching forms; artistic spirit over traditional practicality—these complaints would dog Organic architecture throughout the century. And yet clients remained interested. The Prairie years established a pattern of clientele for Organic architecture. As historian Leonard Eaton has shown, Wright's clients in the Prairie years were largely middle-class, self-made men with an interest in engineering or invention, and women with an original cultural sense. While they were almost all thoroughly suburban family people, belonging to music societies and country clubs, they had no interest in the trappings of social status. Instead of a home of the "right style" (e.g., a Tudor, Georgian, or French Renaissance Revival home preferred by the upper class), they appreciated a home that was practical and efficient, and that reflected their modern technological, business, and suburban lifestyle. These clients were not seeking the latest style of art, architecture, or fashion as set in New York or Paris, and yet their aesthetic desires led to a vivid, cohesive, and dynamic style. This pattern would continue in the clients of Organic architects through the century in small towns like Fayetteville, Arkansas; Scottsdale, Arizona; Midland, Michigan; and Norman, Oklahoma.

The Decline of the Prairie Style

The Prairie style, which first expressed the principles of Organic architecture, faltered around the time of the First World War, along with the Arts and Crafts movement

that was centered in Berkeley and Pasadena, California. American taste moved elsewhere in the 1920s. The popular shelter magazines, now mostly located in New York, stopped publishing Prairie examples.[12] Prosperity sparked people's interest in the traditional taste of the wealthy on one hand and, on the other, an interest in the urban-centered Art Moderne that had been celebrated at the 1926 Paris Exposition.

The suburban Prairie architects lost their focus and fragmented. Their designs lost vitality by 1920. Rivalry undermined the movement, too. A decade after the camaraderie of the shared Steinway Hall offices, Frank Lloyd Wright clearly saw himself as a leader and felt his colleagues would "inevitably repeat for years the methods, the forms and habits of thought, even the mannerisms of [my] present work."[13] His proprietary attitude would hinder the movement in the coming century. In the short run, Wright lost creative interest in the style, ran off to Europe, and then became enmeshed in the ongoing construction of a masterpiece, the Imperial Hotel, on the other side of the world. Returning from Japan in the early 1920s, Wright retreated to Spring Green, Wisconsin. He considered moving his base to Los Angeles. The handful of concrete-block houses he would build there were to be the few he would build anywhere for more than a decade to come.

The fertile partnership of Purcell and Elmslie lost its focus and broke up in 1922. Neither man completed as many strong architectural projects in the following years. Elmslie worked around the Midwest, and Purcell moved to California for his health, designing houses in the Coachella Valley in the 1930s. Shortly after the Mason City projects, Griffin left the United States to oversee the design of the new capitol of Australia at Canberra

in 1914, which largely removed him from the American architectural scene in the same way that the Imperial Hotel in Tokyo drew Wright away. George Maher committed suicide in 1926.

No schools of architecture took up the principles of Organic design. The talent and the institutions that supported it fell apart, and new fashions proved more appealing. It was up to a few scattered outposts to continue the faith and await a revival. Wright employee Barry Byrne (1883–1967) traveled to Europe in 1925, acquainting himself with the latest European progressive architecture at the German Bauhaus and in Amsterdam where Expressionism was flowering. Byrne's 1926 Church of Christ the King in Tulsa, Oklahoma, continued to show a strong expressionist and Modern quality at a time when the young Bruce Goff, precociously talented, designed the Boston Avenue Church in the same city, launching his long career. Wright's son Lloyd and Wright's employee R. M. Schindler had found progressive clients in Los Angeles. Organic architecture was going into hibernation, but the warmth of the Sunbelt kept it alive. •

Hugging the ground, embowered in planters, the Roberts house sits comfortably in the midst of nature. With the glassy walls of the two-story living room letting in the forested surroundings, Prairie houses such as this one in the twentieth century's first decade first articulated the themes of Organic architecture for the general public.

Left, the 1908 Isabel Roberts house (designed by Wright for his office bookkeeper and a family friend) represents Wright's initial interpretations of Organic ideas in architecture. Each architectural element—the brick foundations, the leaded glass window-walls, the flat roof eaves—has a distinct form or material, but they work together to create a unified whole.

Above right, a balcony added by Wright in 1955 juts off the master bedroom.

Below right, the view of the front door shows a very different scale and composition from the front view at left, but the horizontal lines, wood roof line, and flat brick planes relate the many sides to the entire design.

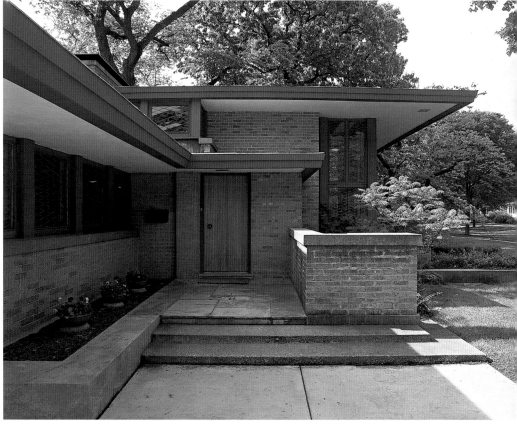

Left, dining room.

Below, windows form a continuous unit that wraps around the corner and unites the two walls.

Right, the living room balances a bold central fireplace and balcony soffits with off-center elements, such as the balcony hallway seen in the upper left of the photo and the doors to the screened porch on the right. Balcony overlooking living room is tucked under the low roof. Colors and textures of natural materials—from the warm tan of the earthen bricks, soft plastered wall planes, and light oak wood trim left unpainted—define the character of the space.

An Organic design can draw on many sources: the geometry of a honeycomb; the expressed warmth of natural wood, brick, or stone; the conceptual integration of large- and small-scale elements into a unified whole. Or, like the Melson house, it can draw from the idiosyncrasies and character of its natural setting. While the standard Prairie house (for example, the Purcell-Cutts and Isabel Roberts houses) uses cleanly chiseled forms and ornament, the spirit of Organic architecture sometimes inspired Water Burley Griffin to use more rugged forms that seem to grow literally from the native rock of the earth.

Left, the Melson house in the Rock Crest–Rock Glen subdivision of Mason City, Iowa, uses the steep, rocky limestone bluff along the Willow River as its starting point. Thus Griffin blends the overscaled voussoirs (a traditional architectural form) over each window and opening with a rough, irregular surface that directly reflects the natural rock.

Above right, the drive-through garage has doors on both sides.

Below right, open balcony extends off the living room. Note the house's ragged silhouette created by the rough-hewn rocks on the corners. Tying house to nature, the house plunges down the bluff to the river like a great outcropping.

Interior finishes are smooth and more domesticated than the primeval, rugged exterior would suggest. Plaster walls, smooth wood trim, and art-glass windows finish the bedrooms on the upper level. Upper left, bedroom fireplace beneath skylight. Upper right, stairs to living floor below. Lower left, bedroom. Lower right, built-in bookshelves fill in the corner pylons seen on each of the exterior's corners. Right, bathroom.

Concrete has long been a favored material for Organic architects. Around 1900 advances in technology made it a strong, flexible material ripe for architectural experiment. But concrete is also fundamentally earthen, a mix of sand, gravel, and lime with the qualities of stone and brick. Here, in one of the earliest examples of an intentionally designed architectural expression of a concrete structure, Walter Burley Griffin shows a view of Organic design very different from his wood-structure houses. He expresses its method of formation: wood forms are built as a mold and then the thick liquid concrete is poured into it, taking the form of the mold. The result is a solid building of flat planes and a flat roof. But his composition of the blocky shapes and his articulation of details begins to reveal the artful side of concrete.

Left, the central two-story pavilion contains the living room on the first floor, bedrooms on the second.

Above right, limestone walls create a platform for the house on a sloping site.

Below right, back side of house with garage at left side.

Next page, an enclosed veranda flanks the house's left side (with an added bedroom on the original terrace above it). The garage is on the right side. Griffin also designed the plan for the Rock Crest–Rock Glen subdivision in which the Blythe and Melson houses sit. Situated along a river, an ideal setting for displaying the themes of Organic architecture and planning, the neighborhood draws from the beauty of the natural setting.

Left, inside Griffin continues the rectilinear forms of the concrete structure in his ornamental elements, such as the tiled fireplace. His leaded window designs add diagonal counterpoints to the lines of the structure.

Above right, dining room.

Below right, thirteen-foot clerestory strip window above the bed demonstrates that the slab roof does not require intermediate supports. Griffin takes advantage of this characteristic of monolithic concrete to introduce an unusual type of window and natural illumination.

William Gray Purcell's own house in Minneapolis reflects the Purcell and Elmslie office's personal interpretation of Prairie-style principles. Though he uses the same bands of art-glass windows, wide eaves, and clean geometrical ornament as did Frank Lloyd Wright, Purcell's composition is more abstract, and the interior spaces more light handed.

Left, the asymmetrical composition balances the jutting living room (mirrored in a small pool beneath the snow) at left with the recessed entry at right. The composition is anchored by the prominent vertical chimney.

Above right, inside the front door, the house divides between the living room, down a few steps at left, and the dining area, up a few steps to the right. True to Organic principles, the entire space is united and yet articulated for each use.

Below right, the living room is slightly sunken into the site.

Above, a small writing alcove with built-in furniture is located in the corner of the living room.
Right, the large living room windows stretch around the corner, creating a glass-curtain wall that allows
the space to appear larger than it is. The fireplace and an original mural by Charles Livingston Bull over
the hearth expresses Purcell's flatter, more abstract aesthetic compared to Frank Lloyd Wright's heavily
modeled surfaces. Furniture was designed by William Gray Purcell.

Left, the main floor is a single unified space defined by a single ceiling plane, as seen from the raised dining area; the living room is several steps below. The living room's lofty volume and banks of windows contribute to the dining room's light-filled spaciousness while maintaining some privacy between the spaces.

Above right, top of stair landing.

Below right, kitchen on main floor.

Above left, bedroom.

Below left, bathroom.

Right, built-in furniture carries through the architectural geometry of the house. In Organic architecture large and small details all express the themes of the design, though adapted to their specific purposes. Note placement of windows at bed height and fold-out desk.

CHAPTER 2
1920–1940

The Younger and Elder Wright

Los Angeles was far enough from the centers of taste making in the 1920s to condemn most architects working there to relative obscurity. However, the city was also far enough away to allow a creative architect to design freely because the conventions of Eastern cities weighed less heavily. Lloyd Wright (1890–1978), son of Frank Lloyd Wright, leveraged this contradiction to keep Organic architecture alive through a dozen years of dormancy elsewhere in the country. The younger Wright created his own distinct interpretation of the Organic ideas he had learned from his father. Not until the late 1930s would the elder Wright reappear on the professional scene with an audacious new version of his Organic ideas and with a trail of followers and adherents to spread them. By 1940, the Wrights and their followers had brought a revitalized Organic design back into the consciousness of the architecture profession.

Frank Lloyd Wright had made an abortive attempt in Los Angeles to revive his career with the design of five houses in the early 1920s, including four using a system of concrete blocks. These homes were a striking departure from the Prairie houses, which were made of wood, stucco, and brick. The Prairie houses were balanced compositions of horizontal roof planes, jutting terraces and wings, and the deep voids of porches and windows, while the

LA houses were made of textured concrete blocks with small, deep window perforations. Yet every aspect of the LA homes followed Organic principles. The rooms flowed one to another through a series of artfully contrived cavern-like spaces. The concrete blocks unified the architecture, performing as structure, ornament, window, colonnade, and landscape foundation. The blocks themselves, manufactured especially for each house, were embossed with rich geometric designs often derived from natural forms. For the steep arroyos of dry Southern California, Wright had created an architecture far different from that which he had designed for the flat plains and forests of Illinois. His message was clear: Organic design could be adapted to new places, new conditions, and new times.

For Lloyd Wright, Los Angeles's bohemian subculture and the lifestyles of Hollywood artists formed the basis of his idiosyncratic career through the Jazz Age. His first wife was an actress and his friends were part of the cultured intelligentsia, which included booksellers, newspapermen, and the like.

Architecture surrounded Lloyd Wright all of his life—as he worked in his father's office, interacted with his father's friends and clients, and accompanied his father on his flight to Europe to escape Chicago in 1909 to work on the Wasmuth portfolio drawings of the senior Wright's work. The relationship of the two temperamental Welshmen was rarely smooth, but Lloyd's devotion to Organic design principles never dimmed.

Lloyd Wright's first house in his chosen home of Los Angeles was a 1921 Prairie house that would have looked right at home on Oak Park's Forest Avenue. But soon the Southern California setting and his own drive to establish an identity separate from his overbearing father led him to develop his own particular expression of Organic design.

His studio and home, built in 1927, had the comfort of a well-appointed cave; his ornament was original and based on crystalline geometries or organic shapes. A dramatic flair that came naturally to Lloyd gave his designs the emphatic presence of a great cataract.

Nevertheless, having talent was one thing, but building a stable career another thing. While Lloyd Wright had his father's imperious prickliness, he did not have the full measure of charm that allowed the elder Wright, with his showman's drama, to attract a steady stream of clients with the means and daring to build. This was a common affliction for Organic architects. While their role model, Wright père, stood bravely and vocally for "Truth against the World" (the Wright family motto), this was not an attitude that helped most architects get jobs. Wright's followers who were not by disposition quiet, retiring, and happy to design as opportunities came along (like the independently wealthy Alden Dow), and who had the burning conviction that they admired in Wright senior took on the world with varying degrees of success. Even so, many architects believed this persona was the only way to honestly live up to the ideals of the Organic movement.

Lloyd Wright's career was long and varied over the decades. His 1926 Sowden house was an Organic design that blended indoors and outdoors and deliberately celebrated nature as the source of Wright's forms. One of his best designs, the Sowden house features an inward-looking courtyard house that turns a remarkable and original facade, like a great yawning cavern, to the city below. Lloyd created the house for John and Ruth Sowden, who were some of his art and Hollywood friends. The rectangular structure was hollowed out in the center for the large courtyard. Blending indoors and

outdoors, the living room and bedrooms of the house all have easy access to the central courtyard with its pool. This exotic space was ideal for entertaining. The courtyard mirrored the historic courtyard homes of Los Angeles's original Spanish pueblo, but it was also evocative of forests, gardens, and even a sacred Mayan space of clouds and thunderstorms.

Due to his clients' more modest budgets, Lloyd often had to work within the constraints of conventional structural systems, yet he used them creatively. The wood frame and stucco Sowden house incorporated custom-designed concrete blocks that convey the Organic theme. The concrete blocks are impressed with abstracted patterns of clouds, plants, and water. Like the abstract cast-stone floral ornament of his father's Hollyhock house, the younger Wright used these blocks to echo the natural landscape of the Southern California site.

The courtyard, clad in the concrete blocks, presented a narrative of natural history. On the continuous lintel that ran above the court's colonnade, the blocks abstracted the shapes of billowing clouds. Rising to support this sky tableau, the columns' blocks were impressed with interwoven trunks and vines of a forest; these columns in turn grew out of blocks impressed with the form of waves and shimmering grasslands.

In other designs of the 1920s, Lloyd Wright explored abstract compositions of blocks encrusted with original ornament. The 1928 Samuel-Navarro and 1922 Taggart houses melded these forms into steep Southern California sites, blending building and topography. Lloyd's ornament of soft naturalistic shapes, impressed in concrete or in copper sheeting, draped over the building like vines.

The Taliesin Fellowship

While the prosperity of the Jazz Age swirled around him, Frank Lloyd Wright spent the 1920s in exile, ensconced in rural Wisconsin with occasional retreats to the Arizona desert. His move away from the centers of power to the wilderness fit his contrarian reputation, but it seemed self-defeating. "Not one reputable architect in ten would know Wright's name, unless as a heretic and wild man," critic Sheldon Cheney reported in 1930.[1]

Struggling creatively for survival and to reestablish himself as the recognized genius he knew himself to be, Wright and his new wife Olgivanna established an arts community (with an emphasis on the Mother Art, architecture) at Taliesin in 1932. Olgivanna in particular knew that her husband drew life and creativity from interaction with followers—especially younger men who were not direct competition. This creative community bore spectacular fruit three years later with exceptional designs for a house in western Pennsylvania; an office building in Racine, Wisconsin; a house for wax-maker Herbert Johnson nearby; and a small affordable house in Madison, Wisconsin.

With these buildings Wright reclaimed recognition for Organic architecture and himself.

Fallingwater, the house in Pennsylvania Frank Lloyd Wright designed for department-store-magnate Edgar Kaufmann, was rooted to the rock ledges, waterfalls, and pools of its site. The curving forms of the Johnson Wax Building in Racine wove its brick walls together into an entire fabric, from minor detail and ornament to massing and plan. The warm wood and brick of the Jacobs small Usonian house in Madison created an environment of natural materials and warmth, not steely, slick mechanical surfaces.

These Wright designs proclaimed that straight lines were no longer the only way to do Modernism. The architectural press and profession were immediately spellbound. Wright, considered a has-been, returned to the scene with a set of Organic forms and ideas that could not be ignored. After the International Style's spare, aloof, mechanistic vision of the modern age, here were shapes that blended with nature, exulted in abundance, and offered a new spatial and structural complexity.

The fruits of the Taliesin experiment lay not only in Wright's startling new buildings but also in his apprentices. Among the young men and women who came to the community, there was a central group of young architects who worked directly with Wright in his drafting room.

Whereas Wright's Steinway Hall colleagues during the Prairie years were his contemporaries, the Taliesin apprentices were contemporaries of his grandson Eric, who was also an apprentice after World War II. Wright called Edgar Tafel, Bob Mosher, and William Wesley Peters the "pencils in my hand" and gave them supervision over his major projects. Some of Wright's apprentices never moved far beyond the vocabulary they learned from Wright; indeed their awe of this master architect, compounded by his imperious manner, stunted some talented architects who dared not stray far from his shadow. But other apprentices who came to Taliesin to live, work, and learn architecture would spread Organic architecture in the coming decades. Among them were Alden Dow, Sim Bruce Richards, Aaron Green, and John Lautner. Lautner, in particular, mastered his lessons and then plunged ahead to create an

expanded vocabulary of forms and spaces based on the Organic principles he imbibed at Taliesin.

Some young architects had trained at established schools of architecture. William Wesley Peters had gone to MIT before Taliesin, and Alden Dow had been at Columbia University's School of Architecture. John Lautner, however, had a degree in English from a state college in Marquette, Michigan, and came to Taliesin to learn architecture from scratch. Wright said he preferred students unwarped by education, but he relied on Peters and others with previous experience. Almost all of the architects had a streak of independence that ranged from youthful idealism, to independent critical thinking, to radical contrarianism.

As an institution to perpetuate the Organic movement, the Taliesin Fellowship—partly Wright's modern architecture office, partly Olgivanna's Gurdjieffian cult and community —was so oddly conceived that it ultimately failed to establish a stable mainstream Organic movement.[2] Perhaps a movement based on individualism, deeply rooted in the philosophy of Emerson and Sullivan, could

Page 39: *Samuel-Navarro house, Lloyd Wright, Los Angeles, 1928.*

Pages 40–41: *Lloyd Wright Home and Studio, Lloyd Wright, Los Angeles, 1927. Left to right, street view, two views of the reception room with Sowden chairs and dining table, living room and balcony, bedroom, street view.*

Page 42: *Taggart house, Lloyd Wright, Los Angeles, 1922.*

never easily become part of a collective establishment. Wright, a complex, often jealous person, was conflicted about enjoying the energy and daring of young architects and fearful of losing commissions or his due tribute.[3] In contrast, the Bauhaus had begun as an official German state architecture school, and the International Style's ties to the American establishment grew when Mies van der Rohe took over the architecture school at the Illinois Institute of Technology and Walter Gropius took over at Harvard, both in the late 1930s. The number of their students alone was far greater than the number at Taliesin and so had a greater influence.

To balance this inequality, Wright vigorously personalized Organic architecture and spent the rest of his life joyfully and pointedly promoting it. The veneration of the individual, a theme that would influence the course of Organic design, added romance to the myth he was telling. The dramatic houses he designed, with daring cantilevered structures in extreme natural settings, encouraged clients to feel they were also daring individuals, set apart from ordinary persons. Ayn Rand raised this attitude almost to the point of parody in her novel

The Fountainhead. This proved a strategic misstep that would keep Organic design out of the mainstream. This stance for individualism largely ignored the mass-built, mass-produced, mass-marketed character of the mid-century economy and culture, even while Organic architecture remained a popular subject of mass-culture shelter magazines. But that was precisely because the Organic architects told a great story about individualism that the average person could dream of, if only rarely fulfill. An Organic house was not like the house next door.

ALDEN DOW

Alden Dow (1904–1983) was a more mature designer than the usual apprentice in the early years of the Taliesin Fellowship. He stayed relatively briefly, but he remained committed to Organic design for the rest of his career.

Dow's father, Herbert, a chemical engineer, had founded the Dow Chemical Company in Midland, Michigan, because of nearby mineral deposits. While the chemical industry had not yet become the giant it would after 1945, the company provided a secure economy for the small city even during the Depression.

Though trained in the full Beaux-Arts method at the Columbia University School of Architecture in New York City, where he graduated in 1931, Alden Dow remained open minded. Eagerly seeking out the relatively few books on Modernism while in school, he admired the work of Frank Lloyd Wright, Joseph Urban, and Paul Frankl. He had seen Wright's Imperial Hotel during a family trip to Japan in 1923, and in 1929 he had traveled to Europe to see the Expressionist brick housing terraces of Amsterdam, an alternative European Modernism distinct from the straight lines of the Bauhaus.

Progressive design attracted the young Alden Dow. His first building, designed while at Columbia, was the Midland Country Club, a clean geometric building reflecting the Art Moderne. A symmetrical pavilion with wings, the building was ornamented with original geometric designs.

Dow first met Wright in 1930 and asked to work with him, but Wright replied that he had no work. Early in 1933, Dow had hoped to work with the great Scandinavian Modernist Eliel Saarinen, then at Cranbrook Academy, another cultured Midwestern art

center, in Bloomfield Hills, Michigan. In May 1933, however, Dow spent several months with Wright shortly after the Fellowship began, and then returned to his home of Midland, Michigan. During his time with Wright, he quickly grasped that there was a point when the influence of the master designer began to prove toxic to one's own design talent.[4]

Independently wealthy, Alden Dow had little difficulty obtaining commissions. He could indulge his love of architecture in a steady stream of houses (often commissioned by Dow executives) and public buildings (often donated by Dow family members.) Yet the acceptance of the Organic style in Midland was not due solely to Dow's prominence, but to the same underlying Midwestern American acceptance of progressive ideas that had brought Sullivan's banks to Owatonna, Minnesota, and Purcell and Elmslie's courthouse to Sioux City, Iowa, a generation before. Not all the Midwest mirrored the closed-minded world of Sinclair Lewis's *Main Street*. Many towns had both a self-reliant remoteness and an educated appreciation of culture and ideas. A respect for the arts was often present in these provincial towns, especially when supported by patrons like Herbert Dow. It was possible for a town or region to develop an individual character even as trains, movies, and Sears Roebuck catalogs created a national culture. This base nourished Dow's career.

After his exposure to Wright, Dow's designs gained a new clarity and ease. Moving from the rigid symmetry of his earlier designs, he became comfortable with freely arranged forms composed in dynamic compositions. In his own studio (designed in 1937) and attached home (added in 1939), Dow created an entirely artificial natural landscape. A dammed river created a small pond as

the foreground for the studio; partly submerged into the water, it rose out of it like a rock. It was not a rock, however; it was a great crystal, its shaft angled skyward, its concrete block structure reflecting a crystalline structure, repeated at many scales, balancing symmetry and asymmetry, and dancing with colors in the light. Inside, the space stepped down through many terraces and slipped beneath the surface of the quiet pond. The studio used a concrete-block system Dow developed in 1934 and repeated in many houses. This system was related, but not identical, to the textile-block system Frank and Lloyd Wright had developed for the Los Angeles houses of the early 1920s.[5] Dow's blocks were a set of parallelogram volumes that reinforced each other and introduced oblique angles to structure and space.[6]

The studio's great angling diagonal roof prefigured the dynamic diagonals of certain Frank Lloyd Wright designs, such as the 1947 Madison Unitarian Church. But the softer ornamentation, and the lack of fussiness in the relationship of the free-flowing spaces make it Dow's own interpretation. The attached residence itself is a complex of related spaces: living room, guest room, gallery hall to the family bedrooms, large master suite with a sitting room boasting its own soaring space. The house rose on tall block walls out of the artificial lake. Dow's Organic house had a relaxed character that contrasted with the intensity of a Wright house. Its asymmetric plan and low profile, which complemented nature, was an early example of many postwar Organic homes.

In the Organic tradition, Alden Dow's work mated science and nature. The residence was picturesque, meant not as an intellectual abstraction of lines but as a sensual, tactile structure, reflecting the lush natural setting

of the Michigan woodland. But Dow was equally interested in modern science as a result of his father's business. He had his father's laboratories at his disposal to help develop plastic products and building applications. Dow also investigated modern psychology to study the effect of color on people. His palette was bright and cheery, not the deep earth tones of Wright. Purples, yellows, and greens activated his spaces. Dow, a lifelong aficionado of toys and toy trains (like Charles Eames and Walt Disney), also had a simple, boy-like character that gave his houses lightness.

The designs of Dow's later career varied in quality. Personal traumas in 1950—the death of his brother, sister, and mother—reoriented his work. Some of his houses were quite simple suburban contemporary Ranch houses, well built but unadventurous. Others were large homes, with the luxuries, drama, and expanse of an expensive custom home for entertaining, for executives like K. T. Keller, president of Chrysler Corporation. After 1950, Dow's office and partners began designing larger buildings, though he continued to design houses until his retirement. The adventurousness of his early designs, however, was diminished, a pattern also seen in some other Organic designers over the years.

PAUL SCHWEIKHER

The apprentices who gathered around Wright at Taliesin formed one cohort of the Organic movement. But Wright's constant self publicizing—providing newspapers with a stream of witty and outrageous quotes, speaking at women's clubs and architecture schools, publishing books, designing and announcing eye-catching projects like a mile-high skyscraper as well as stunningly beautiful and intriguing designs like the Guggenheim Museum—generated a wider following. The architecture profession again accepted him, and many young architects and students at architecture schools around the world came confidently and skillfully to his ideas. One of these architects was Paul Schweikher (1903–1997).

Paul Schweikher moved to Chicago in 1922 and, without any early interest or skills in architecture, found himself drawn to architects' offices. It was a time of building in Chicago; the Tribune Tower, the Wrigley Building, and other landmark skyscrapers were rising. The Chicago School tradition was evident: Sullivan's buildings and Henry Hobson Richardson's Field Warehouse were still standing, but Organic ideas were in decline. Schweikher reported that he was not drawn to these buildings, which only later became iconic landmarks. Once while having lunch at the Cliff Dwellers club, he saw Louis Sullivan across the room but never met him.[7]

Working his way through various offices, Schweikher enrolled at the Yale School of Architecture in 1927 for two years. Traveling in Europe after graduating, he saw the latest in Europe's Modern architecture. A trip to Japan in 1937 took him to the Imperial Hotel, which he admired, and opened him to the distinctive space and structures of Japanese houses. As it had for Wright earlier, Japanese architecture had magnetic lessons for Schweikher. Its use of natural, rugged, textural materials, especially wood and stone, made a profound impression on him, partly because he was color blind. Schweikher found the connection of indoor and outdoor space—another tenet of Organic design—to be impressive. He explained his response to the Imperial Hotel:

The thing that must have impressed me with Wright [at the Imperial Hotel] was the beauty of his overhanging, sloping roofs. The extension of one space into another, done partly by folding screens or the lack of screens, and lower walls, that is walls that didn't necessarily go from floor to ceiling but allowed the passing viewer to look through, if not go through. Wright speaks of spatial differences and I think the Japanese house, palace, or larger scale rooms and spaces give a sense of . . . 'interpenetration'. . . . There's a certain sense inside of the flow of space into itself and also in and out of doors.[8]

In Schweikher's first house, built for his home and office in 1937 in Roselle (now Schaumburg), Illinois, the Japanese and Wrightian influence was seen in long, low lines emphasized by horizontal wood siding, built-in furniture, a massive and simple brick fireplace, and exposed wood beams. Brick and wood walls formed distinct planes that slid past each other. Soft tan brick formed a long horizontal foundation, rising vertically into the chimney as counterpoint. The dark, naturally weathered wood siding, with windows high on the wall, echoed Wright's early Usonian houses. Vertical and horizontal siding and horizontal battens created subtle ornament defining the volumes. It was a new formulation of Organic principles that was distinct from the Prairie style.

Schweikher described his own house in Organic terms: "There was the smell of damp or wet wood, redwood in that case, after a rain. There was the feeling of enclosure in the arrangement of the wings of the house. There was a comfort in the low eaves, feeling that the house belonged to the person in the sense of its scale-relatedness. There was the softness of touch, the warmth of the wood."[9]

The house's profile and open interior spaces paralleled those of Bruce Goff's contemporary Chicago-area houses. Goff moved to Chicago in 1934, where he designed the 1938 Elin and Rant houses in Northfield, Illinois, which used similar brick and wood compositions. The similarity of Goff and Schweikher's Organic designs suggest a reemergence of the Prairie School's Organic ideas in new form. Yet Schweikher was uneasy with comparisons to Goff's work. His unease reflected the general establishment discomfort with Goff's exuberant interpretation of Organicism. Schweikher commented that he was willing to compare his work to Chicago architects, such as "Perkins and Will and George Fred Keck and perhaps Harry Weese." However, he went on to say, "I would hesitate to name Goff. He was somebody to be admired for many different reasons. I don't think he was parallel to us in any way. He was quite independent and not to be mentioned in the same breath."[10]

Schweikher adeptly continued his use of Organic ideas in a series of suburban houses in the years following the war, including the 1949 Herbert Lewis house in Park Ridge, and the W. Russell Scargle house in Glenview. Larger houses allowed him even more range; his 1949 Edward Bennett house in the Smoky Mountains and the 1950 Upton house in Paradise Valley, Arizona, continued his Wrightian explorations. Schweikher remarked, "The [Bennett] house has a strong Wrightian flavor. I think we were all self-conscious about that. I think we wouldn't have hesitated to write to Frank Lloyd Wright and say, 'Apologies,' or 'Hope you don't mind,' or 'We mean it to be a credit,' etc., etc. We all meant it in good cheer and really as a complimentary effort."[11]

The Upton house's assured use of native desert stone embedded into concrete walls is at first glance startlingly Wrightian, and yet on closer examination its composition of volumes and lines show it to be a wholly original Organic design. These distinctions show the flexibility of Organic design in the hands of different architects. Schweikher became a friend of Mies van der Rohe in Chicago, but he never established a relationship with Wright. On the one occasion Wright visited the Upton house, Schweikher reported the reaction of the architect who was both master genius and professional competitor: "As Wright was putting on his hat and cape Upton told me that he said, 'Now Mr. Wright, we've shown you the house. You've been our guest and we've been delighted to have you present. But part of the reason for asking you here was to get your opinion of the work which Mr. Schweikher says was strongly influenced by you. . . . Won't you say something about the house, the architect, or both?' Wright hardly hesitated and said, 'Mr. Upton, you're lucky to have such a fine house by such a poor architect.' That's the end of that story."[12]

Nevertheless, Schweikher acknowledged his appreciation of Wright's architecture: "Wright interested me in his strong emphasis on structural architectural materials, that is, in which the selection of the material itself became a part of the design process. Wood is perhaps the best example in which one sees color, texture, grain, and perhaps in particular, there's a tactile response to. You touch glass and there's little or no reaction, you touch stone, it's cold, concrete, even colder, but wood is always warm, friendly, human."[13]

Like many other architects, Schweikher maintained a foot in both camps of the Modern architectural debates of the post-war period. In 1948 he was asked to join the Congrès Internationaux d'Architecture Modern (CIAM), an international architectural organization dominated by the ideas and students of Le Corbusier, but in

1   Sheldon Cheney, *The New World Architecture* (New York: Tudor Publishing Co., 1930), 198.

2   Kamal Amin, *Reflections from the Shining Brow: My Years with Frank Lloyd Wright and Olgivanna Lazovich* (Santa Barbara, CA: Fithian Press, 2004), 164.

    "I never thought it would turn out this way," Wes Peters said to his colleague Kamal Amin in the 1970s.

3   Robinson, 105.

    Typical of many examples is the break lasting many years between Wright and former apprentice Alden Dow over the commission for the Phoenix Civic Center.

4   Ibid., 9.

5   Ibid., 45.

6   Eventually Dow found the blocks' geometries restrictive, however, and he abandoned them.

7   Betty J. Blum, "Oral History of Robert Paul Schweikher" (The Ernest R. Graham Study Center for Architectural Drawings, Department of Architecture, The Art Institute of Chicago, 1984), 103.

    This contrasts with Bruce Goff, who wrote a letter to Sullivan in 1920 to seek out his advice.

8   Ibid., 131.

9   Ibid., 132.

10 Ibid., 141.

11 Ibid., 176–77.

12 Ibid., 155.

13 Ibid., 143.

14 Cheney, 288.

15 Ibid., 33.

1949 he contributed designs to the Usonia Cooperative in New York, a subdivision of houses by Wright, Wright's apprentices, and other Organic-friendly designers.

After the Upton house, Schweikher's architecture, in partnership with Winston Elting, became more Miesian, the growing mainstream of the architecture profession. He became chair of the prestigious Department of Architecture at Yale from 1953 to 1957 and then head of the Department of Architecture at Carnegie Mellon University in Pittsburgh, retiring to private practice in Arizona in 1969.

The Fall and Rise of Organic Architecture

Schweikher's fence-straddling illustrated how successfully the insurgency of Organic architecture after 1936 took up the battle with the Eastern establishment's International Style for the hearts and minds of the profession. The movement had been virtually dead; in the United States, the professional magazines had largely stopped reporting on Organic design by 1920. Other than a few commentaries by Europeans (such as H. P. Berlage) who acknowledged Wright's early work, there was little memory of the Prairie School through the 1920s. Louis Sullivan's death in 1924 met with little more than passing attention from mainstream architectural journals and critics. Claude Bragdon (1866–1946), a Rochester, New York, architect and theorist, was one of the few observers to pay attention to the Sullivan school in the 1920s. He was instrumental in publishing Sullivan's *The Autobiography of an Idea* (for which Bragdon wrote a foreword) in the year of the impoverished Sullivan's death, a vivid reminder of the decline of Organic ideas. Bruce Goff was influenced in particular by Bragdon's drawings—far more dramatic and unconventional than any of Bragdon's own

architecture—for their geometric ornament. But Bragdon's writings, drawing on Emerson as well as Peter D. Ouspensky, an associate of G. I. Gurdjieff, added a visionary but sometimes unreadable text. Though a strain of mysticism pervaded the early European Modern revolution as well (leading to crystalline forms and expressionist shapes drawn from the human psyche), the clear, rational assertions of the Bauhaus were much more accessible to the architectural profession in the 1920s.

Another rare exception to the lack of critical attention for Organic design was Sheldon Cheney, a wide-ranging observer of the Modern scene from Berlin to Los Angeles, where his brother Charles Cheney helped to develop Palos Verdes Estates in the 1920s. Writing in *The New World Architecture* in 1930, Cheney discussed European architects, such as J. J. P. Oud, Walter Gropius, L. C. Van der Vlugt, Eliel Saarinen, Willem Dudok, Eric Mendelsohn, and American architects Frank Lloyd Wright, Lloyd Wright, and R. M. Schindler; he even mentioned the very early work of Bruce Goff in Oklahoma. Few other commentaries focused on (let alone appreciated) Organic architecture at the time.[14] "The building shall be an organism," Cheney wrote. "Good building is structurally unified and expressive."[15]

But the reemergence of Organic architecture on the eve of World War II added a vital dimension to Modernism. The world was changing. The public and academics were seeking a way to understand the leaps in technology and the way they changed daily life. Organic architecture embraced the machine, but it also kept a firm footing in nature and human culture. Organic design's focus on nature was demonstrated in its contributions to an archetypal form: the house in the wilderness. Beginning with the

mythical Primitive Hut (the Enlightenment's rhetorical invention for the first human impulse to create an artificial shelter), man's relation to nature was a crucial philosophical question. Were humans a part of nature or separate from nature? Was nature an enemy or friend of humans? The craftsmen of Pasadena's Arroyo Seco certainly enjoyed the natural arroyos, wilderness, and mountains at their doorsteps and welcomed natural wood inside, but their chosen homes were still near settled towns and cities. Before 1930 a true wilderness home was most likely to be the rustic cabin of a recluse or a trapper, or the rare intellectual retreat of a Henry David Thoreau. An architect-designed house in the wilderness would have been an oddity, an eccentricity, such as the sybaritic retreat Julia Morgan created for William Randolph Hearst in the remote, enrapturing beauty of San Simeon in the 1920s.

European architects had drawn an unambiguous line between nature and human habitation in Le Corbusier's Villa Savoie and Mies van der Rohe's Farnsworth house. Organic principles, however, encouraged an ideal that used ultramodern engineering to create a comfortable home that blended with a wild place, leaving the surrounding landscape largely unaltered; Fallingwater was the proof. Wright's design blended utter sophistication of design and composition with rock outcroppings embedded in the living room hearth. This blending remained the model for the Organic house, wherever it might be built. In the coming years, as in the Prairie years, most Organic houses would be creatures of suburbia. But they would still embrace that balance of nature and civilization embodied in Fallingwater. •

Frank Lloyd Wright purposely blurs the line between the house and its site by using the same concrete block for the landscape walls and terraces as for the house itself.

Left, the walls that lift the visitor's eyes from the street to the main house are irregular, emerging from of the hillside, and are impressed with an ornamental pattern derived from the natural geometries of leaves and crystals. Where Griffin's Blythe house used poured slabs of concrete formed on the site, Wright uses a system of preformed concrete blocks that he invented with his son Lloyd.

Right, the dappled shadows of trees blend with the light and shadow of the concrete block. Though unpainted, the cast blocks have a rich texture that interacts with the natural setting.

Above left, an outdoor terrace on the upper floor of the house allows residents to step outside to enjoy the scenery and warm climate. Above right, dining room nook has a cave-like character at the end of the well-lighted ground-floor living space. Below, the variety of patterns Wright incorporated into the concrete block of the house demonstrates how he united structure and ornament in one organic whole. The pool was added by Eric Lloyd Wright in the 1980s. Right, living room is lighted by banks of tall windows on two sides. Interior walls are of the same concrete block as the exterior. Pages 50–51, living room seen from balcony.

Compared to his light-filled Prairie designs,
the living spaces in Wright's houses from the
mid-910s through the early 1920s were
frequently darker, more private, and more
sheltered, borrowing from earthen, cave-like
imagery.

Left and above right, bedrooms.

Below right, bathroom opens onto split-level
landing.

After the Prairie style lost favor with the public around 1920, Organic architecture was kept alive by Lloyd Wright in Southern California. He took its ideas in a new direction—spring boarding from his father's ideas into an evocative new architecture of drama and natural images. In the Sowden house, he used concrete block molded into the soft forms of cumulus clouds to shape an opulent autochthonous form bursting forth from between two rational cubes— a powerful statement of natural man in a mechanistic age. In contrast, the Bauhaus was promoting houses that looked like machines in the same years.

Left, the large central window looks out from the living room.

Right, copper gate to front entry introduces the poetic naturalism of the house with its drooping branches and leaves; it displays Lloyd's personal interpretation of the Art Moderne popular in the mid-1920s. The gates lead to a subterranean passageway and stairs that lead up to the front door.

Left above, living room seen from the courtyard.

Left below, sliding doors pull back to unite the living room space with the courtyard.

Right, bedrooms open out onto the courtyard. The courtyard is a poetic evocation of the natural world: the fascia is lined with concrete blocks molded in the abstract form of clouds and the columns are molded in an abstract pattern of leaves, branches, and grass.

Left, fireplace in dining room off living room. Skylight illuminates the dramatically sculpted block.

Below, detail of one of the plant-based patterns of the concrete block.

Right, arcades on either side of the courtyard lead to the bedrooms, kitchen, and an entertainment room.

Left, bathroom contrasts linear Art Moderne tile work with a circular organic skylight.

Right, a very early use of free-form circles in Organic design.

Pages 62–63, the astonishing form of the facade hinted at the lush open-air courtyard at the heart of the house.

Intermingled concrete block and wood trim complement each other in this pleasing composition. Dow studied architecture at Columbia University, which still taught by the traditional Beaux-Art method, before studying with Frank Lloyd Wright at Taliesin. He did not remain at Taliesin long, but the experience dramatically changed his architecture. Though it shares the prototypical flat roof of the International Style houses of the early 1930s, the Hanson house is far richer in forms and detail. It is an expression of Organic design.

Left, the tall windows at center are the living room. The geometric pattern of the gates and fences extending the architecture into the landscape on either side of the house follows the lessons of Frank Lloyd Wright, though the square patterns are unique to Dow.

Above right, the house is composed of rectangular volumes and bands of windows that change on each facade, reflecting the spaces inside the house. The result is a complex design that is tightly knitted together.

Below right, flat plastered planes contrast with concrete block, a system developed by Dow.

Dow integrates different levels to create dramatic spaces; he unites these spaces with the interlocking volumes and trim that run throughout the house. The same technique is used on the exterior facades.

Above left, entry.

Below left, bedroom.

Right, living room. The square corner windows wrapping around the corner help to destroy the boxy regularity of a traditional room and balance the natural light. William Gray Purcell used the same technique in the Purcell-Cutts house living room twenty years before. Dow's system of concrete block used various sizes to create an asymmetrical balance. Unlike Frank Lloyd Wright's concrete-block system at the Storer house with its intricate patterns molded into its surfaces or Lloyd Wright's rounded blocks at the Sowden house, Dow's blocks have a faceted edge that allows blocks to join smoothly like crystals.

Pages 68–69, fence added by Dow associate. Dow frequently used bright, playful colors in his architecture; he believed they had a positive psychological impact on residents.

Wood and brick planes grow effortlessly from each other, with each articulated form contributing to the organic whole. Though Paul Schweikher never worked with Frank Lloyd Wright, the influence of Wright's ideas on the use of natural materials and the relation between a house and its site can be seen in Schweikher's own house and studio in suburban Chicago.

Left and above right, different elements of the house are distinguished by varied wood treatments of flat and board-and-batten finishes.

Below right, horizontal lines and the carport echo the lines of Frank Lloyd Wright's Usonian house designs for affordable suburban housing, first built the year before this house.

Left, living room continues the exterior's wood and brick materials on the interior to create an organically unified design.

Above right, entry hall.

Below right, kitchen. Patterns of wood trim on front door and pass-through shelves are derived from the structure's lines.

Above left, the architect's office and studio are used as an art studio by the current owner.

Below left, Schweikher also designed the house's built-in furnishings.

Right, while the living room is predominately brick, the bedroom uses natural wood for the ceilings, walls, and furniture. While steel, glass, and plain plaster walls were commonly used by the dominant International Style, Schweikher became a master of natural materials and Organic design.

CHAPTER 3
1940–1990

Organic Architecture after World War II

By 1945 Modern architecture had been around for more than half a century. But like many institutions subjected to wartime upheaval, the end of the war sparked a reassessment of the direction of architecture. Creativity, money, and materials, bottled up by war and depression, suddenly found an outlet, and Modern architecture blossomed in a dozen directions. Mass-production housing, custom houses, high-rise offices, urban renewal projects, suburban development, schools, and shopping centers gave architects tantalizing new problems. Architects were suddenly able to explore and build varied ideas and philosophies of architecture (including Organic architecture). The birth of Modernism had provoked experiment and debate; now its reassessment stimulated even more ferment. The wide-ranging results are what we now call Mid-Century Modern.

"During the '50s and '60s when architecture became more tightly organized, the path forked, the Miesians on the high road, the Wrightians on the low road," wrote historian Esther McCoy in 1984. Organic architects were "architectural misfits [who] tripled during the '50s," she reported. "They were often westerners. . . . They knew the land under their feet and what the sky held in store. Some had grown up under the banner of Frank Lloyd Wright."[1]

To Frank Lloyd Wright, the war had been something of a personal affront. No sooner had he been re-lionized by the public and the architecture profession in the late 1930s than Hitler and Roosevelt put his projects on hold and snatched away most of his apprentices. Now with the war behind him, the future was open, and he entered the most productive years of his career.

Like Frank Lloyd Wright, other architects devoted to Organic design saw a bright future and took advantage of the possibilities. Some, including Bruce Goff and John Lautner, took Wright's gospel of originality seriously, treating nearly every commission as a chance to reinvent architecture. Other Organic architects focused on specific themes. For the homesteads of the new suburbia, the sprawling, ground-hugging, multi-winged Taliesin in Spring Green, Wisconsin, became one model for the popular Ranch house in contemporary dressing. For a number of architects, the latest work of Wright was inspiration; his ultramodern homes exhibiting daring cantilevers and dramatic prow-like rooflines gave them license to create a future of exotic beehive geometries, circular pod modules, and plastic-paneled walls.

Later in the century, the futuristic and ever-more-novel technological conceits of Organic architecture buildings (as well as of mainstream Modernism) would fall prey to the fatigue of the new; Post Modernism arrived in the 1970s as an antidote. With pointed irony, the country's leading architecture schools at Yale, Columbia, and MIT invited Bruce Goff to speak to their students in the late 1970s. To mainstream eyes his buildings seemed to represent the extremes of Modernism's fetish for originality—exactly what Post Modernism was opposing. The lack of a middle ground between the two viewpoints remained.

After Goff's death in 1982, the Friends of Kebyar was formed as an association of architects, clients, and historians still committed to Organic ideas. But during the 1950s, Organic Modernism achieved a zenith of design and popularity.

Taliesin and Beyond

In the last decade of his life, Frank Lloyd Wright was at the height of his fame; he was quoted, praised, and contentedly controversial everywhere. Many of his former apprentices had established practices across the country. Apprentice David Henken built a tract of Wright-inspired houses (including three by Wright) in New York, where Wright's "pencil" Edgar Tafel also opened an office. Fay Jones was just beginning his career in Arkansas in the mid-1950s. Partly thanks to Wright's wintertime Scottsdale residence, the booming new city of Phoenix supported unconventional Organic architecture by Blaine Drake, Paolo Soleri, Mark Mills, and a series of other Taliesin apprentices. In California, Lloyd Wright entered one of his most productive periods, highlighted by the 1947 Wayfarer's Chapel in Palos Verdes, California, a dramatic design for a glass-walled chapel on a dramatic cliff. John Lautner was also well launched on his creative and pioneering career. In San Francisco, Aaron Green shared his office with Wright for his California projects. Sim Bruce Richards was established in San Diego.

Wright's influence, however, spread also to talented, often idealistic architects who had not worked with him. In a broad crescent across the Sunbelt, other architects embraced the flexibility and power of Organic design in the decade after the war. Alfred Browning Parker was starting a notable career in Florida, the firm of MacKie and Kamrath had been established before the war in Houston, and Bruce Goff was thriving in Norman, Oklahoma, where he

had a wide-ranging practice and headed the School of Architecture at the University of Oklahoma from 1947 to 1955. In Chicago, Paul Schweikher fit comfortably into the dynamic and varied architecture of that city. In California, George Frank Ligar, Charles Warren Callister, and Jack Hillmer all were inspired by Wright. In the commercial arena, developer Joseph Eichler sought to bring the experience he had enjoyed while living in a 1939 Wright house in Hillsborough, California, to the mass-housing market. Armèt and Davis created a national style by bringing Organic design, complete with garden-like spaces indoors and dynamic, structurally expressive roofs, to the average roadside coffee shop. Even among architecture's high-art establishment, Organic forms were explored by Eero Saarinen, Hans Scharoun, Alvar Aalto, and Oscar Niemeyer, all of whom attacked what historian Kenneth Frampton called the "latent tyranny of the normative orthogonal grid."[2]

In the United States, however, there was a strong nationalist inference to Organic designs—partly a reaction to America's capitulation to the European Bauhaus after 1920. Architect Claude Bragdon, in his foreword to Sullivan's autobiography in 1924, praised Sullivan for, "in the untainted quality of his Americanism, having Lincoln's listening ear for the spiritual overtones amid the din of our democracy, and Whitman's lusty faith in the ultimate emergence into brotherhood and beauty of the people of 'these states.'"[3] Beyond the forms inspired by the natural landscape, the spirit of individualism in the American myth was closely tied to the popularity of Organic architecture in these years.

Suburban Nature

Frank Lloyd Wright focused his own energy on landmark projects: the Guggenheim Museum, the Mile-High Skyscraper, the

Marin County Civic Center, a cultural center for Baghdad, and others. Taliesin fellow John Howe oversaw most of the smaller Usonian houses that the office produced, but Wright was inspired, as he was by Fallingwater's site, by another dramatic site on the rocky coast of Carmel in Northern California for the Walker house. The house would be literally rooted to rocks against which the Pacific pounded—this was a site worthy of Wright's talents.

Most of Wright's houses in his later career, however, were suburban—built in wooded neighborhoods or on gently rolling landscapes, where a swale, pond, or creek served as a setting for a house knitted to the natural scene. Much simplified in detail from the Prairie years, freer in form and the flow of space, these Organic designs were both sleek and opulent. Stone, brick, plaster, and wood combined their tones and textures in a sophisticated, multilayered composition. Hexagonal or triangular geometries regulated the plans, but the site or the client's program could twist the space into unique configurations.

The Walter house in Iowa typifies Wright's custom Organic expression in this period.

Overlooking a river, the house unfolds subtly as it is approached. Wide and solidly set on the ground, a composition of brick walls and jutting roof planes eventually reveal a half-hidden front door. The main room is filled with light from window walls on three sides; the space is wide and open but carefully defined for living, with built-in furniture delineating dining and conversation areas. The space also easily flows past glass walls onto terraces sheltered by wide eaves, punctured by openings to create sun-dappled patterns.

A primary distinction between Wright's houses and those of his mainstream colleagues rests in his use of materials. Wright used natural, unpainted wood copiously. Brick walls form strong, warm planes. Seating, tables, and shelves grow out of these planes, creating their own organic counterpoint to the structure. The structural grid rarely overpowers the carefully shaped living space itself.

This was the spacious, warmly human, site-hugging character of Organic architecture as popularized in *House Beautiful, House and Garden, Sunset,* and other shelter magazines during the 1950s. Many Americans still lived

in houses that were Colonial, Tudor, Spanish, or other traditional styles, but in these magazines progressive designs for modern living offered the architectural equivalent of the dream cars Detroit regularly produced to tantalize consumers. The houses were ideals, though not necessarily most people's actual choice of residence. Some Americans preferred the spare white walls and elegant simplicity seen in the Case Study program of *Arts + Architecture* magazine, but Alden Dow, Bruce Goff, Frank Lloyd Wright, Fay Jones, and other Organic designers were regularly published in the pages of *Life* and other mass-audience magazines, showing the public's interest in these dream houses.[4] Organic architecture was called on for popular movies, including *The Fountainhead* and *North by Northwest,* when an emblem of modernity was required.

Wright's reemergence in the late 1930s introduced a new center of gravity to the architecture community. The influx of European Modernists escaping Nazism had tilted the discussion in America, punctuated by Bauhaus founder Walter Gropius's takeover of the Harvard School of Design in 1938, where he served until 1952, and Ludwig Mies van der Rohe's appointment as

Director of the School of Architecture at the Illinois Institute of Technology in 1938, where he served until 1958. Clear lines were drawn between architects who believed in the house as a machine for living in a sleek, rational, repeatable, and universal form, and the proponents of regional influences derived from vernacular forms and Organic forms. For Organic architects, Modernism was about the unique freedom and ever-expanding possibilities that modern technology offered this generation of architects.[5] Technology was a tool to be used, but not the sole source of form.

The debates grew more pointed as the competing camps struggled for the leadership of the profession after the war. Organic architecture was consistently criticized as intentionally unconventional, self-indulgent, and undisciplined. For example, Talbot Hamlin, a critic for several professional architectural journals, was troubled by the "eccentricities" of the great diagonal roof of Alden Dow's studio.[6] Oscar Niemeyer in Brazil suffered similar criticism for the sensuous, curvilinear lines in the roof of his 1953 house in Rio de Janeiro. In his defense of Organic design, Frank Lloyd

Wright was his own generator of publicity. He spoke regularly at schools of architecture, where the daring and individuality of his ideas appealed to many idealistic young architects. But Organic architecture did not have the strong academic base that the International Style did at Harvard (Gropius's school graduated leaders of the profession such as I. M. Pei, Paul Rudolph, and Phillip Johnson), Illinois Institute of Technology, and elsewhere. Only the University of Oklahoma under the direction of Bruce Goff embraced Organic principles, producing prolific sympathizers like Herb Greene, Bart Prince, and Mickey Muennig.[7]

Wright also cultivated sympathetic magazine and book publishers to publish and promote the ideas. Elizabeth Gordon (1906–2000), editor of House Beautiful from 1939 to 1964, took up the effort with conviction and determination, with the help of John deKoven Hill, her editorial director and a former Taliesin fellow. "Organic unity [is] the living oneness we admire in a tree, a wild flower, in all growing things," wrote the editor of House Beautiful in 1958.[8] For the upscale readership of her magazine, she championed the home of beauty and

taste—and America. In a pointed rejection of European architects, Gordon spoke of the qualities of independence and spaciousness she believed were embodied in Organic architecture. Of course in the middle of the Cold War, nativism was rampant, too. House Beautiful singled out Wright for praise. The magazine made its opinion explicit: before Wright "we were little English men and little French women. We were not yet Americans—most of us, that is. A few were, and they came to Frank Lloyd Wright for a meaningful house."[9]

Elizabeth Gordon contributed greatly to the spread of the Wrightian myth of his singular genius, often at the expense of other Prairie School architects in the historic record. Generously, though, she published many other contemporary architects of the 1950s who followed Wright's line: Alfred Browning Parker in Florida, Aaron Green in California, Fay Jones in Arkansas, Harwell Hamilton Harris in Texas—though not Bruce Goff or John Lautner.

Gordon did not consider European Modernism the only rival of Organic design in the battle for American taste. She carefully stated the progressive argument

against traditional styles—their cell-like rooms and their emphasis on fake facades. In a pointed anecdote in the service of mythmaking, House Beautiful's executive editor during the 1950s, Joseph Barry, recounted Wright's story of witnessing as a teenager the collapse of a classical facade on the Wisconsin State Capitol that killed a worker. The lesson of the story was clear: Classicism kills. The struggle for the American soul and taste was serious business, and Organic architects were the foot soldiers.

Yet despite the struggle, the victory of Organic design was at hand, they felt. "Only today might one say Frank Lloyd Wright has triumphed," wrote Barry in 1958.[10] The raft of architects who had picked up on his ideas, as seen in the pages of their magazine, was the proof. And in the 1950s Organic architecture did indeed seem to be poised to challenge the International Style as the preeminent Modern architecture.

Two Types of Organic Design

Organic design followed two main streams: one followed Wright's lead in form and underlying geometry, and the other began with Organic principles and pushed them

further than Wright usually did. Chief among the latter smaller group were Bruce Goff (1903–1982) and John Lautner (1911–1994).

BRUCE GOFF

The Oklahoman Goff explored and built an astonishing variety of buildings drawing from a deep and imaginative pool of images, organized by a wide and imaginative set of regulating lines. Beginning with Organic principles, he pushed back the boundaries of design. Wright was sophisticated and complex, but Goff's sheer imagination, informed by Modern art, literature, and music took Organic architecture beyond the merely accomplished into the visionary. His houses were hidden realms. Like the entrance to Aladdin's cave through an unlikely doorway, Goff's houses opened into a fantastic space of extraordinary shape and dimensions, of glittering materials and textures that redefined what architecture could be. In the eyes of critics, Goff epitomized the worst of Organic architecture: self indulgence, excess, and lack of discipline. A similar critique had been leveled against the Prairie style. Goff, on the other hand, believed that he was solving architectural problems with an originality born of the freedom that modern materials allowed once stultifying tradition was stripped away. When Mies van der Rohe, the rational classicist of Modernism, said that architecture should not be reinvented every year, Goff agreed; he believed, in fact, that it should be reinvented every month.

The 1947 Ford house in Aurora, Illinois, distills many of Goff's themes. From the exterior, it presents itself as a large, circular yurt. Stepping closer, one sees that it is thoroughly modern, made from the thin steel Quonset hut ribs used by the U.S. Navy's Construction Battalions or SeaBees (with whom Goff served during the war) to create simple and quick shelters; but Goff rethought their possibilities, set them in a circle, tipped them up on end around a common central hub-column, and created a dome instead of the usual Quonset hut vault. The entire structure is set on a low circular foundation wall of anthracite coal, studded with deep blue-green chunks of glass cullet that let light through the wall. The lofty space inside is efficiently arranged into two levels with a mezzanine around the central mast. One segment of the dome is left unroofed, creating an open patio. Rethinking the house according to Organic principles, Goff solves the problem with a totally new space.

The Pollock-Warriner house, on the other hand, shows a very different solution. Based on a plan of nine interlocked diamonds, Goff carefully defined each living space within this fairly rigid geometry. Yet the spaces flow together, with views through carefully contrived windows at the intersections. Pyramidal roofs continue the geometry into the third dimension, and an adjacent screened porch above the garage continues the diamond forms in a lighter, smaller scale. Goff's emphatic, angular crystalline forms recall those of Walter Burley Griffin. Though Wright respected Goff, at times

even he could not follow him. When Goff's patron Joe Price asked Wright in 1953 for his opinion of Goff's first design for his studio in Bartlesville, Oklahoma, Wright dismissed the design, forcing Goff back to the drawing table. Ironically, Wright believed the advanced design would have given Organic architecture's enemies ammunition: "Selfishly, I hate to see the thesis I've worked for life-long in Architecture knocked silly according the prophecies of the too powerful 'opposition.'"[11]

Goff wisely never joined Taliesin, though he was friendly with Wright and invited him to speak at the University of Oklahoma frequently. There, Goff carved out a second center for the Organic movement outside Taliesin. Fay Jones, who was both a Taliesin fellow and a University of Oklahoma teacher, spoke glowingly of the intellectual and artistic atmosphere of Goff's architecture department.

JOHN LAUTNER

By his own report, John Lautner rarely designed buildings during his apprenticeship at Taliesin in the 1930s. He later said he was focused on listening to Wright and on performing the practical building tasks Wright gave his apprentices as a form of instruction. But when the Michigan native moved after five years to Los Angeles in 1938 to start his own office, the results of those six years of listening to the master of Taliesin bore fruit.

His very first houses (such as the Bell residence, which was originally a Wright commission but was turned over to Lautner because of budget constraints) skillfully emulated Wright's forms and vocabulary in the use of brick foundations and wood superstructure, complete with wood trim on the ceiling like in the Coonley house. But Lautner soon broke loose creatively,

as had Goff, taking Organic principles in new directions. Like Alden Dow, he explored concrete-block systems, but when Lautner first delved into poured-in-place concrete in the great curving roof of the 1959 Silvertop house, he found his medium. His architecture was about shaping space, and he found he could do it with the least constraint and most freedom to fulfill his clients' desires by using concrete. In addition, he also built houses out of wood and steel, but in the free-form spaces and shapes that concrete permitted, Lautner found a unique and surprising range of architectural solutions. The Segel, Elrod, Arango, and Pacific houses took an extra step toward perfecting and pushing back the boundaries of concrete design. Lautner did not use plastics as a material.

In his long career, Lautner both gained and suffered from his education with Wright. As an architect, it gave him a remarkably fertile field of ideas that he worked productively for decades; his houses were a unique legacy of creative design that helped shape Southern California architecture.

But as a professional seeking commissions and success, the bombastic character of Wright served Lautner poorly as a model. He shared Wright's self-confidence in design but lacked his skill of dramatic self-aggrandizement. As a business, Lautner's career was uneven. Enough well-to-do clients came along in Los Angeles to allow him to design more than his share of masterpieces, but he was not able to develop the major commissions or large offices his contemporaries like A. Quincy Jones did. Lautner's career is emblematic of the promise and the tragedy that afflicted the careers of many Organic architects who shared an almost religious devotion to its principles.

Architects Who Worked with Wright

In the 1920s Lloyd Wright had been one of the only architects working with Organic ideas. The exotic and varied expressions of the Sowden, Henry Bollman, and Taggart houses and his own studio showed the work of a remarkable, fertile mind. His forms evolved through the decades as Organic design spread after 1940.

The Bowler house shows one of Lloyd Wright's most dramatic designs—an ultramodern Organic house that combined machine-made materials (the roofline is trimmed in blue corrugated fiberglass, the frame is concrete) with rough Santa Maria stone masonry. Planned on a triangular module, walls shift and slide in oblique angles, carrying the visitor through the house; screens and built-in furnishings repeat these angles, uniting plan, space, and ornament in one unified and infinitely faceted theme.

Other young architects joined the Taliesin Fellowship in the late 1930s and went on to solo careers after the war. Aaron Green (1917–2001) was born in Corinth, Mississippi. He was trained at New York's Cooper Union architecture school, where he first heard of Wright. He visited Wright's 1937 Ben Rebhuhn house in Great Neck Estates, New York, and was impressed. When he returned to Florence, Alabama, in 1939 he gained a commission for a house from newlyweds Stanley and Mildred Rosenbaum. So confident was he of Wright's abilities that he convinced his clients to hire Wright instead of himself. Contacting Wright, Green served as liaison during construction, and Wright offered him an apprenticeship. After World War II, Green set up his own office in Los Angeles, and then moved to San Francisco in 1951. He kept in touch with Wright, however, who established his West

Coast office with Green there. They worked together on several projects, including houses and the Marin County Civic Center.

Sim Bruce Richards (1908–1983) was "one of a small band of architectural dissenters," wrote historian Esther McCoy.[12] Born in Oklahoma, Richards was one-quarter Cherokee. Trained as an artist at the University of California at Berkeley, Richards was an artist, muralist, and weaver, as well as an architect. Before graduating, he left for Taliesin in the 1930s at Wright's request. Settling in San Diego after World War II, he began a steady career of modest-sized buildings, including houses, churches, and small civic buildings. His own house on Pt. Loma—one of several he designed for his family—is a wood structure that wraps around the edge of the hill.

Young architects continued to flock to Taliesin in the early 1950s to work under the famous Wright. Arkansas-native Fay Jones (1921–2004) was one of these, having received degrees in architecture from the University of Arkansas in 1950 and Rice University in 1951. He taught at the University of Oklahoma under Bruce Goff, and then was at Taliesin for less than a year in 1953, after which he moved back to teach at the University of Arkansas.

The influences of both of Jones's mentors, Frank Lloyd Wright and Bruce Goff, can be seen as he worked out his own design aesthetic in Stoneflower, a 1965 vacation home in rural Eden Isle, Arkansas. The stone walls of the ground floor built into the sloping site are Goffian: their rugged and serpentine walls create carefully designed caverns, with built-in ledges as benches, and include a bathroom with a waterfall shower. Skylights bring in filtered light from above. The upper floor and loft, however, are made of wood in striking contrast. Here the wood

structures and delicate wood tracery of straight firm lines first seen in the Prairie houses is reinterpreted as a forest of wood trusses that creates an intricate three-dimensional ceiling. A wood deck, exaggerated in length, thrusts out over the slope toward the lake view. In this design Jones reenvisions his mentors' ideas, while pointing the direction to his own trademark use of wood trusses in numerous chapels later in his career.

Jones's 1964 Pine Knoll house in Little Rock, Arkansas, on the other hand, is more specifically Wrightian. A modernized interpretation of the Taliesin in Wisconsin, it is "of" the hill, wrapping around the brow, not "on" it. Its gently framed courts and decks blend inside and outside spaces seamlessly. Jones mastered the subtle and even fussy aspect of Wright's designs in the careful placement of columns, one in juxtaposition to the other, thereby shaping spaces, linking one room gracefully to another and subtly directing the eye to the view. The offset ashlar stonework is neater and less ancient in appearance than Wright's. Jones's stonework creates an effective texture over the house's foundation walls and pillars. With an open carport and low, wide gables, the house demonstrates the fine line between many Wrightian designs and the contemporary Ranch house then popular in suburbia nationwide.

Eric Lloyd Wright (b. 1929), son of Lloyd Wright, visited his grandfather at Taliesin as a boy during summers, and then became an official apprentice from 1948–1956, excepting service in the Korean War.[13] After his apprenticeship at Taliesin (where he worked, among other projects, on the concrete prefabricated Usonian Automatic houses his grandfather built in the 1950s), he moved back to Los Angeles and worked with his father. He now has his own office

in Malibu on another typically Wrightian hilltop site.

Architects Inspired by Wright

Excelling in Organic architecture, however, did not require studying under Wright. Houston's MacKie and Kamrath became one of the most prolific firms working in the Organic idiom. Houston in the 1940s and 1950s was growing and in need of architects. That boom—and the laissez-faire attitude that lead to Houston's refusal to institute zoning codes—might have indicated infertile ground for a firm with a strong design sensibility. Likewise, the local cultural elite's interest in the Miesian aesthetic, imported via Phillip Johnson and carried on ably by local architect Howard Barnstone and others, might have indicated a lack of sympathy for Organic design. But MacKie and Kamrath had a long and successful career designing custom homes, hospitals, public housing, places of worship, drive-ins, office buildings, and corporate headquarters. On a smaller scale, Alden Dow had a similar impact on Midland, Michigan, and John Lautner and Lloyd Wright hoped for such an impact on Los Angeles. Though limited to the Texas region, MacKie and Kamrath were the most successful Organic architects in terms of the breadth, number, and quality of their buildings. Organic architecture became a noticeable presence in Houston.

Both Fred Mackie (1905–1984) and Karl Kamrath (1911–1988) attended the University of Texas at Austin, though they met in Chicago. Oklahoma-born Kamrath received his degree in 1934. He had first been impressed by Wright's work in publications he saw in the University of Texas library. Moving to Chicago to work for the Modernist firm of Pereira and Pereira, Kamrath met MacKie, who had graduated in 1928. Chicago had been hard hit economically by the Great Depression, so

the pair decided to move to the more prosperous Houston to start their architecture partnership in 1937. Kamrath was to handle design, MacKie project management.

Kamrath finally met Wright in 1947 at Spring Green, Wisconsin, and then hosted him at the 1949 AIA Convention held in Houston, where Wright was given the AIA Gold Medal. The young Fay Jones also met Wright at the same convention as the master architect spread his influence through the South.

Kamrath's Houston home demonstrates his firm hand in using the Organic vocabulary as well as his inventive abilities. The cross-shaped house has a long bedroom wing—children's rooms at one end, master suite at the other—intersected by the living room/dining room/kitchen wing. The house sits on a rise above Buffalo Bayou; as the land falls away, the house is cantilevered out to achieve its floating character. The crisp, asymmetric gable roof over the cross wing is a signature Kamrath shape.

After 1970 the firm grew larger and accepted more institutional commissions. As with Dow and some others, the inventiveness of the design became watered down; though the designs continued to be Organic, they became less original. Kamrath designed a church and an office building as overscaled versions of Unity Temple as late as 1974, just as Harwell Hamilton Harris (1903–1990) designed residential versions of Hollyhock house in the 1950s.[14] The diminution of originality contrasted with the continuing innovation of form seen in John Lautner's later work.

Another architect equally skilled in applying the principles of Organic design is Alfred Browning Parker (b. 1916). As a boy, he

Page 77 left to right: *Pacific Coast house, John Lautner, Southern California, 1990; Stevens house, John Lautner, Malibu, 1968; Turner house, Aspen, Colorado, 1982.*

Page 78: *Paul house, Aaron Green, Palo Alto, California, 1952.*

1 Esther McCoy, "Sim Bruce Richards," *Nature in Architecture* catalog, San Diego Natural History Museum, April–June 1984.

2 Kenneth Frampton, *Modern Architecture: A Critical History* (London: Thames and Hudson, 1985), 202.

3 Sullivan, 5.

4 For Dow, see *Life* (March 15, 1948); for Goff, see *Life* (March 19, 1951).

5 Amin, 29.

6 Robinson, 145; *Architectural Forum* (April 1941).

7 As a rough estimate of the relative strength of mainstream versus Organic Modernism after the war, the 1945 book *Tomorrow's House* by George Nelson and Henry Wright featured ninety-six architects; six can be identified as Organic designers. Of course Nelson and Wright were identified with the mainstream camp.

8 Joseph Barry, *The House Beautiful Treasury of Contemporary American Homes* (New York: Hawthorn Books, Inc., 1958), 20.

9 Ibid., 11.

10 Ibid., 12.

11 David G. DeLong, *Bruce Goff: Toward Absolute Architecture* (Cambridge, MA: The MIT Press, 1988), 126.

12 McCoy.

13 Bruce Brooks Pfeiffer, ed. *Letters to Apprentices: Frank Lloyd Wright* (Fresno, CA: The Press at California State University, Fresno, 1982), 117.

14 See Mackie and Kamrath's 1974 Emerson Unitarian Church and 1974 Big Three Industries Building, Houston, and Harris's 1955 Stevenson house, Fort Worth.

15 Jan Hochstim, *Florida Modern: Residential Architecture 1945–1970* (New York: Rizzoli International, 2004), 62.

16 Charles Jencks, "Bruce Goff: Michelangelo of Kitsch," *A.D. Profiles* 16, Vol. 48, No. 10 (1978), 13.

moved to Miami in 1924 with his family. He graduated from the University of Miami in 1939 and then studied architecture in Sweden and Mexico. After service in World War II, he opened his own practice in 1946. He never studied with Wright, though he invited Wright to speak at the University of Florida, where Parker still teaches. Wright praised one of Parker's houses with one of those trademark compliments that also managed to praise himself: "This Florida house aims at the highest goal to which architecture may aspire: Organic architecture." Also impressed was Elizabeth Gordon of *House Beautiful,* who spotlighted the home as one of the featured Pace Setter houses.[15] That 1953 four-level house used the landscape, sloping to Biscayne Bay, to create four staggered levels, including a roof terrace and studio. The contrast of solid stone piers (built of an overscaled ashlar pattern of local oolitic limestone), which anchor long, flat cantilevered concrete floor slabs, is strikingly Organic. The two living area floors are enclosed with a light continuous screen of windows framed by wood (and covered in louvered doors for ventilation in the Florida climate). The design combines site, climate, and local materials to tie the house to the ground; the shape, structure, and plan evolve from the site and the client's needs. Inside, the varied levels allow space to intertwine, creating distinct places while uniting them as a whole.

Organic theory bestowed on architects the freedom and license to explore a wide range of forms and structures. This was the case for Charles Haertling (1928–1984) of Colorado. Born in Missouri in 1928, Haertling was not pointed to architecture after an inspiring visit to a Wright building, but rather after taking a Navy aptitude test that indicated his talents. Graduating from Washington University in St. Louis on the GI Bill in 1952, Haertling moved to Boulder,

Colorado, beginning his own practice in 1957. His houses ranged over the variety of Organic types, from the Wrightian Willard-Shapiro house in 1961 to the curvilinear Brenton house of 1969. In the latter, Haertling used an innovative concrete-gunite structure shaped over forms into rounded shapes.

The Experimental Nature of Organic Design

An awakened interest in environmentalism in the 1960s echoed the themes of Organic architecture. Always drawing on the natural setting for its inspiration, often using sun, wind, and earth to shape its form, Organic architecture was philosophically in sync with the ecological movement. The architecture of counterculture communes in the 1960s often borrowed the free forms and naturalistic imagery of Organic design; the iconoclastic, antiestablishment attitude of both movements often overlapped. Many of the counterculture houses were built by nonprofessional designers using recycled materials, often outside the view of building-code enforcers. They came to be identified as "wood butchers." Though sometimes expressing a native genius for form and ornament, these hand-hewn structures were often lumped together by critics with the sophisticated complexity of a Bruce Goff house.[16]

The freedom to explore new forms, varied images, free-flowing spaces, and new materials marked the course of Organic design. This resulted in an astonishing range of forms and plans, of aesthetics and attitudes. Wright himself worked in deeply complex, carefully elaborated geometries, all the while maintaining strict control over structure and landscape. He carefully considered the placement of each wall and column in relationship to each other wall and column in a design. Many of Wright's followers,

however, did not feel the same compulsion for control. Beginning with a few structural or spatial themes, John Lautner, for example, allowed the flow of function or landscape, the framing of landscape views, and the free play of the structure to shape his spaces. The same variations can be seen in the use of curvilinear shapes in Organic design. These curves were not the perfect geometries of traditional Roman or Renaissance architecture, which were intellectual abstractions of Platonic geometry. When Wright used circles to organize a plan in the 1938 Ralph Jester project, they were more like the lines of nature: the shapes produced by the ripples of a handful of pebbles thrown in a pond organized into functional rooms and outdoor spaces. Bruce Goff would take such forms even further in the Ford house, creating a three-dimensional hemisphere. Then taking Claude Bragdon's suggestion of the nautilus shell, Goff's Bavinger house became a three-dimensional spiral corkscrewing up out of the Oklahoma landscape, its rooms suspended from the structure. The powerful waves of the Pacific became the roofs of houses by John Lautner—from the Stevens house to the Segel house. Though many critics, accustomed to the rational grid organizing space, could not comprehend the order behind such free-form architecture, these irregular shapes did, in fact, have their own rules. •

One of the most daring and inventive Organic architects, Bruce Goff experimented with unconventional materials and bold geometries to create his spaces.

Left, the circular Ford house places a shingled, domed roof atop a foundation of anthracite coal. Green glass cullets peppered in the black wall let colorful, jewel-like light into the interior. The orange steel columns are Quonset hut ribs tipped on end to create the yurt-like form. Carport is at right in the picture.

Above right, at the peak of the dome, the curving steel ribs rest on a central structural mast, where a skylight draws attention to their intricate moiré pattern.

Below right, garden side of the house. The smaller dome contains a bedroom. Where the full Quonset ribs are exposed, a screened porch cuts into the house.

Above left, a herringbone pattern of wood unifies the interior of the hemisphere dome. Curving ribs act as columns separating spaces.

Below left, dining area around the perimeter of the main space. Note the green glass cullet in the coal wall.

Right, at the center of the dome sits a sunken kitchen area and a raised mezzanine above. Goff combines varied and opulent textures for the skylight, wood ceiling, and ashlar coal walls in this single space.

Left, dining, music, and library spaces are arrayed around the sunken conversation area defined by the built-in curving sofa. Models of other Goff projects are displayed in the edge of the mezzanine. Above, photo of Bruce Goff.

Above left, the end of the living room is glass where a section of the dome is cut out for the screened porch.

Below left, a small dome contains a bedroom. The soffit overhead is lined with rows of rope—another unusual material for which Goff discovered an architectural use.

Right, the lip of the circular mezzanine above juts out over the sunken conversation area. Note the color of the natural light coming through the glass cullet in the wall.

The Mossberg house represents a late Frank Lloyd Wright design that reinterprets the Prairie house by using the simplified lines of Mid-Century Modernism. Its massing, gently pitched gabled roofs, large central window, and ornamental trim echo the 1902 Susan Lawrence Dana house, and its brick-pillar structure echoes the 1904 Darwin Martin house, but the broader stretches of glass and cleaner, less elaborate ornament and forms reflect the simpler forms that Wright apprentices, such as Alden Dow, had adopted earlier. This clean, contemporary use of natural materials and engagement with the natural setting marked Organic architecture in the 1950s.

Above right, glass dominates the living room wing, which faces the southern sun, on the garden side.

Below right, the house's north side, the entry approach, is more opaque. Wright incorporated the natural drapery of plants and vines as living ornament on his houses.

Above left, the living room is a two-story composition of brick planes and walls. Where the Prairie houses placed the all-important hearth at the center of the room, Wright creates asymmetrical arrangements of solids and voids. A balcony from the bedroom floor above overlooks the living area.

Below left, the dining room backs up to a solid brick wall and faces out to the garden through a window wall.

Right, living room. The materials are unpainted brick and natural wood; the site is a suburban forested lot; the structure of brick pillars and planar walls is articulated and defines the interior spaces. The ceiling line is accentuated with strips of wood, and the angle is repeated in the simple divisions of glass in the main window.

The organic integration of the house's space is seen in these views of the stairwell.

Left and right, the cantilevered treads, suspended on metal rods, are open to the space.

Below, upstairs the mezzanine landing is open to the living room.

Left, the approach to Karl Kamrath's own house presents a balanced composition of wood, brick, and planting. The garden is at the house's right; landscape-architect Garrett Eckbo was consulted on the design.

Above right, the bedroom wing offers each room a garden view. Though the use of broad horizontal wood planks on the cantilevered deck are similar to Frank Lloyd Wright's use of the same material at the 1939 Sturges and other houses, Kamrath brings his own crisp sense of proportion and detailing to his designs.

Below right, opposite side of bedroom wing reveals clerestory windows, providing more privacy to the side facing the main entry.

The bedroom wing forms one axis and the living room/dining room/kitchen form a second axis in this cross-shaped plan.

Above left, view from living room toward dining room and kitchen; front door is at the left. Kamrath used this distinctive asymmetrical gabled roofline often.

Below left, front door.

Right, main entry hall looking out to back terrace. Updating the Prairie architects' use of leaded glass windows, Kamrath creates a simpler composition out of the same elements of glass, wood frame, and art glass.

Left, a view of the inside of the same living room bay. Above, the large living room bay juts out over the garden. The house sits on a promontory above Houston's Buffalo Bayou.

A compact house that brings the warmth of natural materials to a living space, the architect's own house nestles into its hilltop site but also provides expansive views of San Diego in the distance.

Left, living room wing has glass walls on two sides.

Above right, the master bedroom is in the angled prow at left.

Below right, street side of house is modest and serves as a backdrop to the landscaping.

Unpainted wood is used throughout the house. Above, the simple plan combines kitchen and dining and living rooms in one space.

Left, master bedroom.

Right, living room.

Pages 106–7, street side of house has few windows, following the pattern of Frank Lloyd Wright's Usonian houses.

Strong geometries and a hyperrealistic use of materials create extraordinarily vivid spaces in Bruce Goff's architecture.

Left, the roof's clustered, crystal-like polyhedrons are echoed in the steel canopy clad in blue-green corrugated fiberglass panels that shelter the terrace atop the garage.

Right above and below, the flagstone landscaping also repeats the angles of the shingled structure, uniting the house and setting.

Goff remodeled the interior for the current owners in the 1980s. Above, the open plan's extensive space can be seen; nine interlocking squares, set at ninety-degree angles to each other, create the single large interior divided (except for the bathrooms) only by movable partitions. Right, the pyramidal roofs bring the ceilings down almost to the ground. The windows are the leftover infill between roof structure and floor rather than traditional openings in the walls.

Left, kitchen. Spaces are defined by specific furnishings and light from skylights at the top of each pyramid roof form. Above, a bedroom is defined by one of the diamond-shaped spaces. Chamfered corners become windows or doorways. Folding partitions that provide privacy can be seen at the far left.

At Silvertop, John Lautner uses advanced building technologies in the service of a natural habitat. The house responds sensitively (and boldly) to its site.

Left, the audacious concrete roofline arching over the living room is a shape borrowed convincingly from the surrounding hilltops. The imagery is far from the flat-roofed, mechanistic appearance of many Modern houses.

Above right, the steep driveway arrives at the front door. Designing the interior spaces first, Lautner had little interest in creating an impressive traditional facade.

Below right, the house's two wings push aside to create the central hilltop open as a courtyard. The living room, gently sheltered by the arching concrete roof, is essentially a space as open as the natural hilltop itself.

Pages 116–17, the snaking, cantilevered driveway is partly covered by a large vine-covered trellis, left.

Above, an atrium just inside the front hall never allows the visitor to forget the natural setting. Right, the living room is a free-flowing space that subtly encourages the experience of relaxing, conversing, and dining. Lautner uses curving lines for the ceiling, fireplace, and walls to gently define spaces.

Left, the frameless sheets of glass offer the least intrusive division possible between indoors and outdoors. At far left, part of the glass window-wall moves aside mechanically on a track to literally blend inside and outside.

Right, the pool is a few steps from the living room.

Brick, wood, and glass are the simple materials creating the atmosphere of this hilltop house in Los Angeles's Silver Lake district. The third generation of the Lloyd Wright family to build in Los Angeles, Eric Lloyd Wright learned his architecture from summers with his grandfather, a stint as a Taliesin apprentice, and years working with his father, Lloyd Wright.

Left, the compact house expands into the yard with its pool—and also extends further to the view of Silver Lake and its hillsides in the distance. The design is one large space, with interlocking roofs defining the bedroom and living room at the side of the main pavilion.

Above right, the central space with high ceiling is flanked by two lower wings.

Below right, view from the living room with Silver Lake in the distance. Landscape is welcomed inside with a planter on either side of the glass window.

Above left, the kitchen sits behind the brick fireplace wall.

Below left, the house's space can be flexibly divided with a movable screen to separate the bedroom from the living area.

Right, the living room with the open fireplace on the far wall; the dining area is to the left.

In the hands of Colorado architect Charles Haertling, Organic architecture takes varied expressions reflecting structure and site. In the Willard-Shapiro house, a light wood frame rises from a solid concrete-and-stone foundation.

Left, the house's living room commands a panoramic view as it juts out over the hill. The master bedroom is on the lower level.

Above right, from the parking area, a long arcade approaches the front door and allows for a leisurely enjoyment of the view seen from the observatory-like living room at the end.

Below right, seen from the living room, the linear design emerges from the hillside. The design maintains the natural hillside vegetation. The lower floor contains the bedrooms, sheltered from the wind behind concrete walls.

Pages 128–29, the living room explodes outward with its gabled roof and wood-frame skeleton, distinguishing itself as a blossom distinguishes itself from the tree on which it grows.

Above left, to the right of the fireplace, the space flows into the dining room.

Below left, fireplace at the opposite end of the living room.

Right, the living room with mahogany paneling. A low horizontal soffit maintains the unity of the space while the angular geometry of the ceiling and glass window-wall act in counterpoint. Uniting diverse spaces, the ceiling is a consistent presence throughout the main floor of the house.

Left, visitors pass by the study and its outdoor patio along the walkway down the long entry arcade leading to the front door.

Right, the dining room with the family room and kitchen beyond.

An exotic orchid of a house in color, detail, and extravagant presentation, Lloyd Wright's design draws on a wide range of images to create its unique architecture.

Left, the triangular geometry is carried through in the angled openings of the deck railing and emphasized by the translucent blue plastic corrugated panels lining the upswept roof. This translucent fringe lifts the house visually—a theme underscored by the cantilevered terrace that looks as though it is floating above the ground.

Right, inverted columns reiterate the diagonal lines of the deck railing. Though counterintuitive (the stone columns stop short of the roof), steel columns provide the necessary structure while lightening the visual presence of the house.

Above, furniture and ornamental screens designed by the architect continue the angular forms of the structure and roof. Right, different areas in the open living space are defined by the stone columns and united by the open filigree work of the ornamental screens.

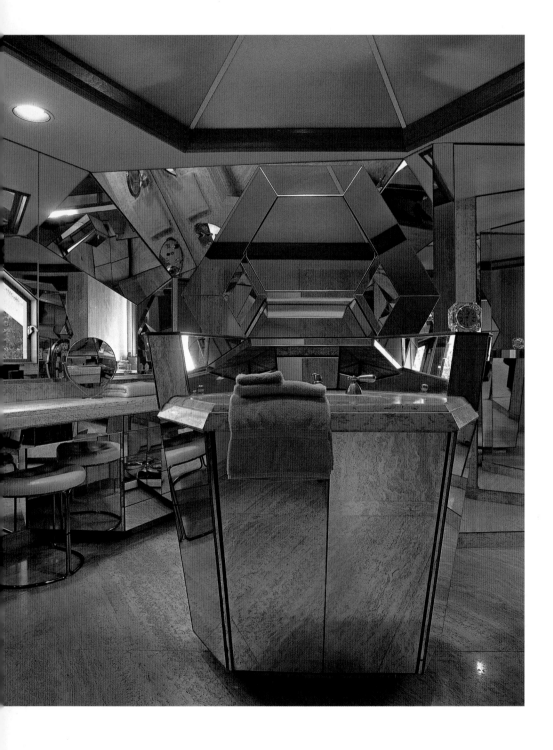

The master bedroom is on the upper floor. Left, the master bathroom's faceted glass surfaces dematerialize the space. Above top, the sitting room overlooks the living room. Above bottom, a bedroom opens to an outdoor terrace on the upper level. Right, sitting room. Trained by his father as an architect since he was a boy, Lloyd Wright developed his own distinctive vocabulary and geometries for his Organic designs.

Fay Jones was one of many architects deeply influenced by Frank Lloyd Wright's Taliesin in Spring Green, Wisconsin. Here, Jones uses Taliesin's design vocabulary of ashlar stone walls, rooted in the earth, contrasting with broad, hovering roofs that repeat the lines of the horizon. The stone walls marry the architecture to the rise and fall of the rolling landscape.

Left, entry.

Above right, the entry porch introduces spaced stone pillars to both separate and connect the spaces.

Below right, the living room looks out toward a river plain below.

Right, hugging the ground, the house's stone structure rises out of the earth to support the great roof.

Above left, in a classic example of Organic design, the same stone walls that slowly grow out of the ground continue inside. Like Walter Burley Griffin's Melson house in Mason City, Iowa, Jones uses the rugged pattern of geologic strata as a texture for these walls. Jones's ornamental wood doors and light fixtures mark the special nature of the entry.

Center left, Jones opens most of the end wall of the living room with glass. Such a feat would have been impossible in the Prairie era, but mid-twentieth-century architectural engineering allowed for this striking unity of indoors and out. The stone, the lines of the decorative wood window frame, and the colors of the living room also help to blend the architecture with the natural environment.

Below left, the irregular placement of stone pillars and the fireplace shapes the flowing space of the living room, which has an openness that links to the entry and dining area. The wall to the left of the fireplace has built-in shelves and seating, which unify the structure and the furnishings.

Left, view of the galley kitchen. By mid-century, the kitchen was no longer a separate room for servants but an active part of family life and the architecture itself. Jones brings the same care in designing decoration and windows to this space as to the other public spaces.

Above, kitchen. Note the indirect lighting from soffits and clerestory windows.

Above right, bedroom. Ornamental elements create a more elaborated, generous architecture than the minimalist Bauhaus interpretation of Modernism allowed.

Below right, bathroom.

Frank Lloyd Wright's Prairie houses often thrust walls and terraces out into the landscape to claim nature as part of house. Above, right, and pages 148–49, Jones continues that tack in these screened structures and flagstone steps and terraces. Right, rough stone walls and smooth stone paving complement each other. The small fountain echoes the verdant Arkansas landscape.

Fay Jones carried on the principles of Organic architecture in the late twentieth century. In Stoneflower, a vacation home in the rolling Arkansas hills, Jones explores a design that melds the two Organic traditions he was exposed to: the earthen, expressionist, curvilinear tradition of Bruce Goff and the light, geometric, wood tradition of the Prairie style.

Left, a tall, thin wood volume with living and sleeping area rises from a stone foundation, which contains a cave-like lounge and bathroom. The foundation is partially hidden behind the brush. The cantilevered deck extends from the living room out over the sloping landscape.

Above right, entry is via the stone ground floor. Skylights letting natural light into the rooms in the lower level can be seen at the left of the wood structure.

Below right, the deck extends out into the treetops; ornamental braziers are an example of Jones's original decorative designs that carry out the theme of the architecture in smaller details, as they did in the Prairie houses.

Above left, lower level has an irregular, cave-like stone wall that transforms into built-in seating. Floors are flagstone, and outcroppings become tables in this evocation of the forms and materials of nature. As this level is wider than the upper level, skylights bring in natural sunlight on either side. Spiral stair leads from entry to upper level.

Below left, grotto bathroom directly evokes the natural stone outcroppings of the region.

Right, main floor has a contrasting wood structure and wood trusses that echo the vertical lines and canopy branches of the natural forest in which the house sits.

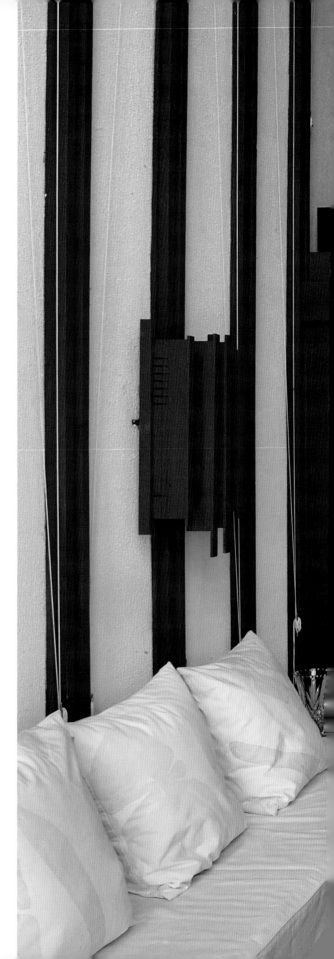

Left, the vertical proportions and elaborate wood structure of this house established a motif in Jones's work that he employed in his later career designing religious structures.

Above right, open sleeping mezzanine looks down on dining area.

Below right, sleeping loft. Jones reinterprets the Prairie-style aesthetic of thin wood sticks against white walls in this small home. The exaggerated proportions of the main room and the elegance of the carefully chosen architectural elements mark Jones's personal adaptations of Organic concepts.

While some Organic architects specialize in exploring the possibilities of one or two materials, Charles Haertling explored a wide range of materials and their appropriate forms. The polyurethane structure of the Brenton house takes a radically different shape from the wood-frame Willard-Shapiro house he designed in 1961.

Left, street view shows rounded, contiguous forms inspired by the way barnacles naturally cluster. The front door is under the raised pod, which was Dr. Stanley Brenton's study.

Above right, a central concrete foundation core was poured with flat concrete platforms for the several floor levels. Steel-wire mesh was then formed over the platforms and polyurethane was sprayed over it to produce the rounded shapes.

Below right, each pod was individually framed on site, with some incorporating two floors, some one floor. Six pods are arranged radially to take advantage of views.

Left, circular stair on middle entry level leads up to the study above and down to the family rooms on the lower level. Above, rooms lead radially off this central hall.

The Organic polyurethane structure required that windows and other conventional architectural elements be reinvented for the Organic design.

Above left, views like this of Boulder, Colorado, determined the placement of pods. This view from the raised study shows the other pods arranged around the central skylighted hall. Haertling creates clerestories at the edges of the pods to balance natural light in the main public spaces.

Below left, spiral stair to lower bedroom level.

Right, some windows are treated as the voids between structural elements, above left, or as circular openings formed in the steel reinforcing mesh.

A river and a forest run through this Florida home, built by the architect for himself. Set in a grove of palm trees, the design takes every opportunity to open views of the tropical vegetation.

Left, the entry winds up steps and through outdoor enclosures whose vertical columns echo the tree trunks around it.

Above right, the house's three pavilions are wood frame, lifted off the forest floor on concrete pylons and placed at angles to each other, creating outdoor terraces between them.

Below right, deck terrace over waterway.

Left, exterior paneling of bleached Honduras mahogany is milled to reflect the scale of slender palm fronds that are the natural environment of the house.

Above right, the living room's rosewood spiral stair leads to a bedroom on the upper level.

Below right, top of entry stairs seen from the living room. The fountain pours into the linear pool winding between the structures.

Left, above and below, the master bedroom is in the treetops. Stair to the master bedroom is enclosed with glass. The door and mirror at right are a later addition to the design.

Right, the fountain seen on the previous page pours water into the long pool that winds between pavilions. In Florida's lush tropical landscape, the outdoor walkways become practical living spaces that also connect the house's three pavilions.

A house free from the strict, predetermined grids of conventional building systems can respond to the rhythms of the residents and the site.

Left, the beachfront Segel house combines concrete towers with laminated wood beams to contain the spacious, light-filled rooms of the house.

Right, front door.

Pages 170–71, the complex curve of the living room ceiling sweeps down to a free-standing fireplace and an outdoor garden beyond the glass walls at right.

Above, the irregularly shaped living room includes smaller, more intimate areas off the main space. Right, dining area windows look out to the beach. The architecture combines the embracing sense of a cave with the warmth of wood and the light allowed by glass.

Left, master bedroom on the second level is equally free form in plan. Though such Organic designs have been criticized as "undisciplined," Lautner's use of light and expansive space in the service of human habitation is in fact intentionally designed in every detail.

Below, slatted skylights allow light to flood the center of the house.

Right, bedroom is terraced with several levels, a design that echoes a natural landscape.

Above, studio includes a transparent glass floor. The composition of curving concrete forms and warm wood ceiling is emphasized when the windows are left as the simplest kind of infill between solid forms. Right, pool and garden off of living room.

Though Aaron Green used elements—like broad roofs, natural wood, concrete block, original decorative flourishes that resonate the architecture's lines—as did Alden Dow, Frank Lloyd Wright, and other Organic architects before him, Green interpreted them in a distinct manner. In this house from his mid-career, his forms and ornament are simplified but still organically integrated.

Left, the pointed prow of the broad roof emphasizes its horizontality. The unassuming front door is at the right of the garage doors.

Above right, rear of garage wing. Angled light monitor at far end brings light into the living room. Green uses a standard split-face concrete block with integral color in large planes.

Below right, the wood detailing of the roof soffit and the cast-concrete window surrounds add visual punctuation as a contrast to the simplified lines. The house was designed for the architect's son.

Left, view from hall back through front door. The main public spaces are contained under a single high gable ceiling. Natural wood and stone, used to draw attention to the house's inherent beauty, form the decoration of the house.

Above right, a system of columns, concrete fireplace, and built-in cabinets divides the corridor space from the living spaces.

Below right, atrium greenery brings the outside indoors.

Above, living room at left is defined by low built-in conversation area. Right, dining room and kitchen beyond. Flattened triangular forms are repeated in the ceiling, fireplace, and chandelier. The dining table chairs are Frank Lloyd Wright designs.

Left, concrete-block corner pillars flanking bedroom windows perform their job of holding the lintel running around the ceiling of the house. The built-in cabinets form a block beneath the molded-concrete window surrounds. Art-glass clerestory window repeats the lines of the low roofline.

Above right, office and atrium.

Below right, bathroom.

CHAPTER 1990–PRESENT 4

Organic Architecture Today

A century after Organic architecture blossomed in the big cities and small towns of the Central Plains, its possibilities and exuberance still appeal to many architects and many clients. Over those hundred years, Organic design moved steadily westward from the rolling hills of Wisconsin and plains of Chicago to the dry hills and austere deserts of the Southwest. The architecture, ever reflecting its natural setting, changed, too.

Today, the promise of exhilarating forms shaped by imagination and desire (not simply the logic or limits of a structural system) can be seen in the dramatic reinventions of space and contour by Frank Gehry, Thom Mayne, MVRDV, Rem Koolhaas, and others who now lead the mainstream closer to the Organic ideal of free form.

Frank Gehry discovered his kinship with Bruce Goff, one of the purest Organic architects, late in his career. Gehry commented, "I knew of Goff in my architectural beginnings as a shadowy mystical figure in Oklahoma who made bizarre buildings . . . [but] Goff talked about the intuitive in a way that I find familiar. His discussions about connecting to the other arts, to music and painting, are more areas of coincidence. He expressed an interest in the precarious, pushing ideas to their limits. He talked about awkwardness, irresolution,

and the unfinished. These are all issues and ideas that move me also." Echoing Claude Bragdon's assessment of Sullivan and Elizabeth Gordon's of Wright, Gehry also said of Goff, "He was an American. Like Wright he was the model iconoclast, the paradigm of America. He was of the American conscience, the antidote to Gropius's pontifical European presence." Of one Goff masterpiece Gehry observed that "the Ford house is interesting because it utilizes a ubiquitous World War II form, the Quonset hut . . . to make a personal, elegant space within a rather awkward silhouette."[1]

Noting Walter Gropius alongside Goff, Gehry pinned down the two opposing views of Modernism, never quite equal, that coursed through the twentieth century. Gropius's mainstream Modernism had originally promised a spirit of invention and newness to break the bonds of convention and tradition; in time, it became a formalized style itself. The long line of Organic design presented an aesthetic that tapped into many facets of the American national character and landscape. It was about abundance, breadth, color, texture, complex geometry, and an opulent range of source imagery, whereas the Bauhaus and its progeny were a severe, spare, simple, elegant composition of machine images: straight lines, flat surfaces, and a cardinal devotion to the machined structure as its central guiding motif. The Bauhaus was centered in the dense, cultured cities of Europe, while Organic architecture drew its creativity from remoteness and nature. The mystic usually did go out into the wilderness.

The respective strategies by which each Modernist philosophy propagated itself were as different as their respective aesthetics. The Bauhaus aesthetic began as an official design school and then was adopted in America by the establishment academies, museums,

journals, and the corporate power structure at the heart of the economy. Organic architecture, rooted in the individualism of Ralph Waldo Emerson, Walt Whitman, Louis Sullivan, and Frank Lloyd Wright, employed a single dramatic individual to put forth its story. This strategy did make an impression on the larger culture—and helped its architects to get jobs, that essential duty of any architect. Organic's stance of opposition to the conventional wisdom kept it a minority view but also a constant counterpoint.

The two sides of Modern architecture were ever at odds. For those of the mainstream's minimalist sensibility, the abundant silhouettes, ornamental geometries, and compound textures of an Organic house were seen as excess and ultimately dismissed as "kitsch." Critic Charles Jencks spoke of Bruce Goff as having the courage of his own bad taste. But Goff's architecture must be recognized as a coherent aesthetic choice, albeit often one of mystery, transcendence, and the sublime. There is still something bizarre about Goff's designs. And that is good. They push the boundaries of conventional logic. They stretch our expectations, show what is possible, and challenge us all to continue to explore the frontier.

The Practice of Organic Architecture

Some Organic architects are inspired by the natural setting to blend their buildings into rocks, fields, hills, and lakes. Others use those images metaphorically, echoing the landscapes of nature—of caves, meadows, and forests. Others are inspired by the abstract principles of a natural structure—drawing inspiration from the way a tree integrates strong trunks, hidden widespread roots, and delicate leaves into a single unity. Some architects are inspired by the literal shapes of flowers, birds, bones, and crystals.

Many use modern methods of construction and engineering not as an end point but as a tool to achieve their goals.

Reviewing the last century, Frank Lloyd Wright remains the mainstay of Organic architecture. His houses are often (though not always) carefully preserved, books on his designs form a cottage industry, and his reputation is established. But it is significant that among the most successful of today's architects associated with Organic ideas, most trace their influences to the two strong and committed mavericks who did keep exploring the frontier—Bruce Goff and John Lautner.

In this chapter, we present only a few of the current practitioners. Mickey Muennig and Bart Prince both studied with Goff. Helena Arahuete was John Lautner's associate for many years. Wallace Cunningham studied at Taliesin in the late 1970s, but he left after eight months; in Southern California he became acquainted with Lautner. Ken Kellogg, on the other hand, has been as consistently and directly true to the rebel spirit of individualism itself as Frank Furness was in the 1870s when Louis Sullivan admired his work. Goff and Lautner grappled with Organic concepts and took them beyond Wright's forms. As Muennig explained, Wright "got stuck somehow in a particular mold, but Goff kept on going."[2]

One of the weaknesses of the movement (though not of the designs) was the peculiar organization of the Taliesin Fellowship. In the 1930s, it had resurrected Wright and the movement in spectacular fashion; it was Wright's office and home, created and crafted to support him with a community of followers to constantly refresh his creativity. But it was also the creation of his wife, Olgivanna, Taliesin's cofounder, and it fulfilled her desires for a social community to lead

according to the principles she had learned under the mystic philosopher and teacher G. I. Gurdjieff. A peculiar insularity grew up in their realms at Spring Green and Scottsdale under Olgivanna's direction, especially after Wright's death in 1959.[3] The flame was kept alive but was sputtering. The institution developed at Taliesin to promote Organic design was not going to be a help then; the movement as it had been organized was going to require the energy of individual architects to keep it going.

Over the last century, the careers of Organic architects had varying trajectories. Often as much a religion as a profession, a career in Organic architecture put extra stresses on a designer. Wright's career was a roller coaster, ending on an upward arc. His reputation has only risen since his death. Many Organic architects labored in Wright's shadow. Many mastered Wright's forms but went no further—their creative impulses dying out with time and changing fashion. Much of the work of Alden Dow became

more conventional after the 1960s, as his office and partnership took on larger buildings. Dow spoke poignantly in later years of the "loneliness of living in one's own creation for forty years."[4] Rugged individualism had its price.

A few Organic architects maintained their creative vitality to the end. John Lautner and Bruce Goff had prepared early in life for a career rooted in independence, underscored when they established an amiable

professional distance from Wright. Some of Wright's former apprentices grew in different directions, gaining energy from the stimulating battle to remain original. Fay Jones taught at the University of Arkansas, which allowed him to limit his commissions to those that interested him.[5] Inspired by vernacular barns as well as forest canopies, he developed the use of ethereal stick trusses in rectilinear, upright buildings that were quite different from his earlier sprawling houses tied to the earth.

As the real estate market and the architecture profession changed by the end of the twentieth century, most middle-class clients could no longer afford to hire an architect. Almost all custom residential architecture, of whatever style, increasingly required wealth. For example, early in John Lautner's career in the 1940s and 1950s, he demonstrated that he could convey tremendous imagination in smaller, often owner-built houses. Those opportunities did not come his way often in his later career, however; his office instead relied on large houses with lavish budgets. With those resources, he could freely explore his structural imagination. His houses appeared more frequently in the sumptuous pages of *Architectural Digest* than in the mainstream professional journal *Architectural Record,* demonstrating the once-again widening division between Organic and mainstream Modernism.[6]

This economic fact led to the perception of Organic architecture as the province of a limited segment of the society, which disregarded the broader social role of architecture. Today this pattern holds: the architects we have selected to represent the latest examples of Organic design often build custom homes in exclusive communities. The economics of homebuilding have changed, but the aesthetic philosophy that all things are possible is still alive. The following designers are among those who prove today that any architecture that can be imagined can be built.

Organic Architects Today

Mickey Muennig (b. 1926) began his education as an aeronautical engineer at Georgia Tech but soon transferred to the University of Oklahoma to study with Bruce Goff, where his education included "reading fairy tales, looking at Japanese prints and

listening to music by Debussy and Ravel."[7] Muennig remembers the times Wright came to lecture: "I was just awed by him. He came into the auditorium in his cape, and everyone cheered. He had the forms and proportions in his buildings in beautiful harmony."[8] Muennig settled along the rugged Big Sur coast of Northern California, a striking natural scene that has inspired his design work there. In addition to the many houses he designed, the upscale Post Ranch Inn, with bungalows that nestle in the cliff side and stand high on stilts in the forest, is also located there.

The work of Wallace Cunningham (b. 1954), while rooted in Organic ideas, has taken many directions in the San Diego area. In custom-home design, the desires of the client are paramount for Cunningham. For the son of Mies van der Rohe's client for Chicago's Lake Shore apartments, Cunningham created a rectilinear set of tall, thin boxes on a narrow in-town lot, sliced open at the end to create shafts of light. The unity of the spaces created by the many slender boxes acts in effective counterpoint to the linear vertical slices of spaces. Other Cunningham houses use unconventional engineering to create soaring organic shapes on cliff-side sites. His signature buildings show expansive spaces united with a firm grasp on structure. Cunningham says his approach is "more intuitive than intellectual" and often related to "a distinctive feature of the site. . . . I try to tap into the psyche with unexpected manipulations of form and light, which are intended to be as sculptural as they are architectural."[9]

Helena Arahuete worked for John Lautner for twenty-five years. The Belgian-born, Argentina-raised architect studied engineering and architecture and mastered concrete construction, a common material in South America. Her father's friend

Leonard Malin, Lautner's client for the famous Chemosphere house, suggested she work for Lautner, and the association began in 1971. When Lautner died in 1994, Arahuete completed several of his projects.

While Arahuete is an unassuming person, she is a self-assured architect. The site of the Roscoe house is more than Wrightian, it is Roarkian—the kind of Master of the Universe mountain-top site in Northern California that Ayn Rand's hero from *The Fountainhead,* Howard Roark, would have embraced. With views stretching from the Golden Gate to the Sierra Nevada Mountains, the 13,500-square-foot house presses the boundaries of construction, combining deep-rooted concrete piers and enormous glass windows on a site subject at times to 100-mile-per-hour winds. The phenomenal glass opens the site to the natural panorama that spreads in all directions and can be seen from almost anywhere on the main floor. The swimming pool, which cantilevers out over the hillside, is a muscular gesture of willed weightlessness. In the hands of Arahuete, the character of the house emerges from the hilltop site and from its strong concrete structure as a uniquely articulated form. The design seems as inevitable and natural as a crystal in a granite matrix or a blossom bursting from a branch.

Bart Prince (b. 1947) was a close associate of Bruce Goff. His work continues the sumptuous, opulent love of texture, form, and color that Goff revealed in materials both rare and ordinary. "Let the site read through," Prince says. In the Mendocino County house, the softly curving lines echo the landscape. The inland wind and the ocean view determined the shapes of the house. Price comments that "I always start with the actual program—how it fits on the site. It sounds mundane, but makes sense."[10]

Prince thus points out a common fact about Organic houses: for all their unusual design, they often work well for the clients. Their peculiarities in the eyes of others derive from the original answers to practical problems that the architect invents. Prince, in fact, considers the term *Organic* dangerous. Many assume, he says, that an Organic house is something "indistinguishable from nature"; to the architect, however, it refers to the way a building is conceived and how parts relate to each other as parts of the same organism.

Ken Kellogg (b. 1934) is a San Diego native who began his architecture career at age eight, building structures from wood found along the beach near his home. He attended the University of California Berkeley, the University of Southern California, and the University of Colorado, but his actual education came elsewhere. More than any architect of his generation, he turned his career into a brave search for form.

The design of Kellogg's high Desert house near Palm Springs, California, mixes natural forms with advanced technology—as Organic houses have since the Prairie style. Like Arahuete's Roscoe house, the desert house is a concrete structure. The house has a distinct form with shapely pillars that taper into overhead canopy roofs. In this corner of the American Southwest, the forces of cataclysm and erosion have heaped up enormous rock boulders in great naked piles. The house's columns and roofs echo the curving boulders, shaped by wind, water, and the ages. The columns take their soft tan luster and nubbly, un-burnished textures from the living rock. "The house enhances the site," says Kellogg.[11]

The Desert house is essentially one large room that steps down the hill on several terraces. The master bedroom at the top

Page 187: *Psyllos house, Mickey Muennig, Big Sur, California, 1985.*

Page 189 left to right: *Brad and June Prince house, Bart Prince, Albuquerque, New Mexico; Price house, Bart Prince, Corona del Mar, California, 1984; Hight house, Bart Prince, Mendocino, California, 1993.*

1 DeLong, ix–x.

2 Lucie Young, "The Nabobs Love It and Rough It," *New York Times* (May 6, 1987).

3 Amin, 149.

4 Robinson, 136.

5 Ivy, 8.

Jones built more than two hundred houses in his career.

6 In another irony, the Prairie style, vanquished in 1920, was revived by real estate developers and residential architects in the 1990s as a highly popular high-end residential architecture.

7 Young.

8 Ibid.

9 See www.wallacecunningham.com.

10 Bart Prince, interview with Alan Hess, September 1995.

11 Ken Kellogg, interview with Alan Hess, November 2004.

12 Ibid.

13 Ibid.

overlooks the spaces below. The interstices between the mushroom-cap pillars are filled with glass, bringing in clerestory light throughout the space. The house is thus an extension of the natural desert floor, with modifications for shade and human comfort. The imagery is organic: skeletal, desiccated, austere, and yet shapely and beautiful.

Like a powerful lens, the design focuses the sublime vastness, the teeming life, the diamond-hard wildness of the scorching wilderness. It also makes it a part of the daily life of the home's residents, two successful visual artists and their son. The design contradicts expectations about concrete buildings as opaque and massive, defined in Walter Burley Griffin's 1913 Blythe house discussed in the first chapter. In Kellogg's design, concrete plays an essential role in protecting the residents against two of the California desert's most merciless features: earthquakes and heat. The reinforced concrete pillars resist seismic jolts, but rather than taking the form of a massive pillbox, the design is sensual, agile, filled with sunlight, and surprisingly comfortable as a home. "Let the doors open at night," explains Kellogg, "and that keeps the temperature neutral all day."[12]

The heat stored in the dense concrete during the day radiates out to warm the house at night. Cooled by the time morning arrives, the concrete absorbs the sun's rays slowly and the air inside remains temperate. The house does not require the usual refrigerated air-conditioning. Instead, efficient swamp coolers extract enough moisture— even in the parched desert—to cool the air.

The conventional architectural categories don't apply to a house that resolves both practical and aesthetic questions with this much imagination, study, and reinvention. Natural metaphors spring to mind to describe it: bleached bones, a cluster of enormous mushrooms, stalactites and stalagmites, insects. But the truth lies deeper.

The house, in Kellogg's telling, designed itself. "Once you see the site and take it in, it's a feeling you know is going to happen."[13] Any Organic architect for a hundred years might have said the same. Kellogg's design in the early twenty-first century internalizes the spirit of a hundred years of Organic designs. It reflects the elements— the sun crossing the sky, the inevitable earthquakes, the sublime desert landscape. Cutting-edge construction technology allows free rein to the imagination of the client and architect unhindered by preconceived shapes or forms. It transcends simple rationality to tap deep currents of human culture and intuition. •

The craggy Big Sur coast offers Mickey Muennig a spectacular natural setting to draw on for the design of his own house.

Left, on these windswept slopes, Muennig partially buried the main house in the earth, allowing the native planting to cover its roof.

Right and pages 192–93, the house turns a circular gateway door toward the Pacific Ocean. A foyer with pivoting glass doors offers flexibility whether the weather is stormy or pleasant. Circular trunk-like forms and branch-like trellises borrow from natural forms and blend the house into the landscape.

Left, the central atrium holds a lush Edenic garden at the heart of the house in contrast to the more rugged landscape outside. Above, the living spaces of the house, including this low arched fireplace and living room, circle the garden atrium.

Left, the square atrium (seen here before the current vegetation was planted) is set in the middle of a circular space and topped with a steel-framed skylight that can be moved aside.

Clockwise from the upper left: front door, fireplace, kitchen, and workspace.

Right, present-day view of atrium looking toward front entry.

Left, workspace. Other rooms lead off the large central space. Above, kitchen. Skylight above cutout arch balances the light in this mostly underground house.

Above, the backdoor leads out to an outdoor court sheltered from the wind. Right, the house nestles into the hillside overlooking Pacific Ocean. The atrium's skylight can be seen in the center of the sod roof.

Nearby, Muennig built a glass pavilion as part of his home.

Left, Big Sur view.

Below, doors open to the air.

Right, workspace beneath the mezzanine, reached by ladder at left.

Pages 204–5, this interpretation of Organic architecture virtually disappears into the landscape.

The soft, curving lines of this house draw attention to the gentle lines of the Idaho hills.

Right, aerial view shows the relationship of the central living area and flanking wings. The snaking road reflects the native topography.

Pages 208–9, exterior corridor wraps around the concrete block wall of a bedroom wing, bringing a panorama of the landscape and the house itself into view. Prince uses natural lines to unite his house to its surroundings instead of setting it apart, as did International Style Modernists.

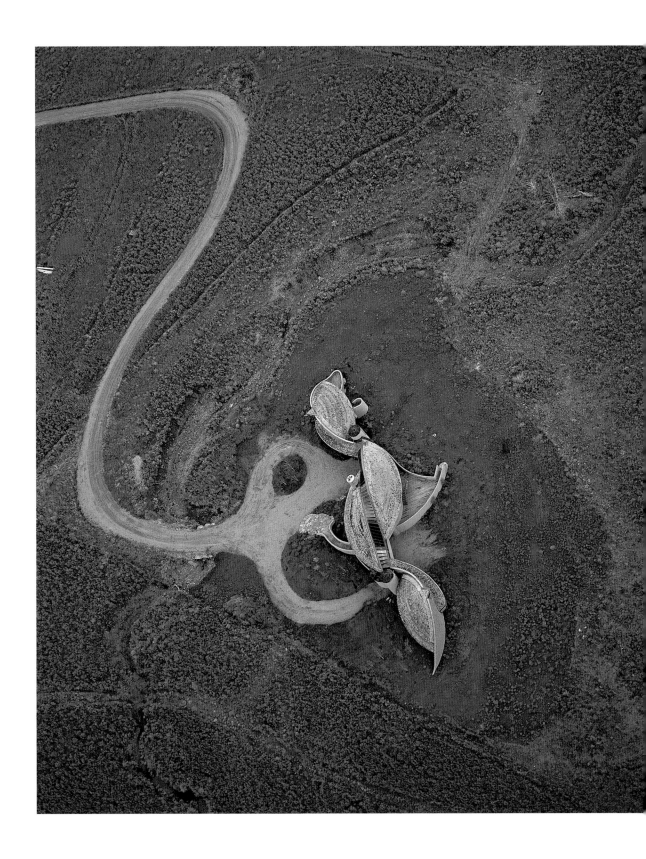

Left, a skylight runs down the spine of the central living area.

Above right, the lines of the built-in sofa follow the lines of the exterior architecture.

Below right, corridor. The house expands into both vertical and horizontal dimensions.

Above left, the house's structural skeleton is exposed, strengthening the serpentine forms of the architecture. Built-in furniture also plays its role in shaping the spaces.

Below left, kitchen.

Right, each element contributing to the curvilinear structure—steel diagonal supports, wood rafters and shingling, concrete foundation walls, and flagstone floor—expresses its individual character but also creates an organic wholeness.

Left, ramp from valley floor to house raised above the surrounding valley floor.

Below, bathroom.

Right, sitting area. Prince takes advantage of the complex architecture to allow light into the house. The wood chair in foreground is a Frank Lloyd Wright design.

Pages 216–17, though the house's shapes echo the surrounding hills, the house design does not disappear into the landscape. Instead, its organic lines draw attention to— and even enhance—the beauty of the natural setting.

Expressions of Organic architecture are as diverse today as a century ago when the architectural style produced examples as dissimilar as Frank Lloyd Wright's glassy Roberts house and Walter Burley Griffin's stone Melson house. True to the tradition, the Skilken house seems both primeval and high tech; the forms are astonishing and curious. But like most Organic designs, the house emerges from the natural setting and from an evolutionary method of organizing space and interrelating structure.

Right, ornamental elements on the house and property elaborate on the themes of the design.

Above, the roof's metal cladding takes on a sensuous character in its lines and colors.
Right, abundant landscaping blends the house with the land and the forest.

Working in a visual vocabulary of curving lines, Prince uses arching wood posts and radial beams to create the intersection of spaces inside the house. Above, an inward-looking landscape of stone walls and wood ceilings is arranged to suggest a space that is continuous and without an obvious endpoint. Right, living room. Though entirely designed, the architecture evokes natural forms and space. Below, view of house from lake. Instead of using steel and glass to create rectilinear shapes, Prince invents softer forms suggested by the landscape.

Left, individual spaces are defined by oval frameworks beneath the sheltering canopy of the roof.

Right, clockwise from upper left, several levels are visible in the large open space; often multiple colors, textures, and patterns form the sumptuous spaces in Organic architecture, as in the stairway; kitchen; stairway supports rise out of stone foundations.

Left, glass, water, and plantings combine to create this Organic space.

Below, Prince unites vertical spaces as he does horizontal spaces.

Right, water wraps around stem-like structures. By expanding beyond the usual conventions of Modern architecture that use the sharp-edged forms of the machine for inspiration, Organic architecture draws on a wide range of images. This freedom to build literally outside the box demonstrates the tremendous plasticity of Organic design.

A century of Organic design has encouraged the liberating architectural exploration seen in this design. It is another demonstration of the flexibility of concrete, traceable to the experiments of Walter Burley Griffin and Frank Lloyd Wright in the 1910s. As a plastic material, concrete is shaped as much by the architect's imagination as by functional structural demands. This house uses concrete, glass, water, and space to create its own natural environment of cliffs and slopes, lakes and peninsulas.

Left, the front door leads to a central courtyard.

Above right, the main floor opens to outside terrace.

Below right, the spiral ramp encloses the courtyard. The tall door in the wall at right enters below the level of the pool of water. Water, a natural material, takes on a distinct geometric volume that blends with the other architectural forms.

Above, with the main living spaces lifted above the ground, the ground plane is free to be landscaped for outdoor living. The structure takes advantage of modern engineering to create strong, daring shapes, but it is not a slave to that technology. Modern materials are used in the service of the creative living space and nature. Pamela Smith was the interior designer, George Sultanyan was the structural engineer, and Guy West ran the project in Cunningham's office.

Above left, stair.

Below left, kitchen and dining areas.

Right, living area on second level. Concrete follows different, freer design requirements than steel. The regular modular rhythms of a steel structure usually define regular, rectangular spaces, but concrete allows the architect to arrange spaces as open landscapes responding to the site, the views, and the lifestyle of the residents.

Pages 234–35, bedroom and terrace.

Left, bedroom.

Above right, bathroom. The sunken bath becomes part of the house's landscape environment.

Below right, bedroom looking out to the terrace.

Above, entry and main door. The parapet spirals up as a ramp around the central courtyard. Right, view of courtyard from inside the main door.

The Roscoe house's angular concrete forms and cantilevered structure use concrete in a markedly different manner than the Desert house by Ken Kellogg (page 254). The differences illuminate how Organic designs are distinct from each other. The designs grow organically from the specific site, client, and materials. Whereas Ken Kellogg uses the free-form, curvilinear shapes concrete can achieve, Helena Arahuete uses concrete's great strength to create a glass house on a challenging site.

Left, atop a mountain that commands views from the Golden Gate to the Sierra Nevada Mountains, the Roscoe house redefines the archetypal glass house in strictly Organic architectural terms. The cantilevered deck holds the house's swimming pool.

Right, the front entrance and its terrace look south toward San Francisco Bay.

The plan of the house is circular, with one space leading into the next. Above, the 360-degree views can be seen from anywhere in the house's main floor. The lower floor, sunken into the hilltop, is a sheltered space that looks inward to its own garden atrium. Right, living room. The studied simplicity of the architecture utilizes large expanses of glass, wood, and stone with a sure sense of scale to create a house that matches the expansive landscape around it.

Left, the house's lap pool juts outward over the hillside and also extends into the house. Large glass doors slip aside to connect indoors with outdoors when the weather permits.

Above right, the water's surface is repeated in the surface of the bay beyond.

Below right, individual wedge-shaped roof structures shelter the indoors. The clients asked the architect for an angular rather than a curvilinear house.

Above, kitchen. Right, dining room with kitchen beyond. The wood ceiling fixture contains sound and light systems and improves the general acoustics in the house.

Left, master bedroom on the main floor. The other bedrooms are on the lower floor, along with a library, exercise room, and glass-walled garage.

Above and below right, the two master bathrooms have clerestory windows. The concrete structure and steel-framed roofs supported on the intermittent concrete pylons allow interior partition walls to be low.

Above, kitchen at dusk. Right, dining room at night. The frameless glass walls, engineered to withstand the hilltop's high winds, disappear at night, leaving the focus of the architecture on the concrete pylons that support the roof and the warm flagstone plane of the floor. Pages 252–53, master bedroom at dusk. The glass walls eliminate any sense of separation between indoors and outdoors. Stone paving also blends the natural setting and the human habitation into one unified whole.

With its bone-like roof structure laying on the dry desert landscape, the house evokes one obvious aspect of Organic architecture: these forms seem drawn directly from the site's weather-rounded formations. But the design is more than picturesque. The inventive structure and single flowing interior space grow inventively from the demands of the site and client's lifestyle.

Left, the house sits halfway up a rubble-strewn hillock in California's Mojave Desert.

Above right, Organic architecture has long been interested in the possibilities of concrete. Here, a series of individual reinforced concrete columns, rooted in the earth, flare out in wide canopies. The spaces between the canopies are filled with glass, bringing light into the center of the house.

Below right, the colors, shapes, and textures of the concrete roof sections tie the house to the dramatic desert site.

Pages 256–57, steps lead up to the main entry between the mushroom-shaped concrete structures that combine columns and roof.

In his architecture, Kellogg avoids conventional structures and forms, preferring to invent forms to solve the particular requirements of the project. Left, concrete columns act as part of the house's passive solar heating and cooling system. The concrete mass absorbs the sun's heat slowly during the day, keeping the house cool during the heat of the day. At night, the stored heat radiates into the house, moderating the cold desert nights. Standard refrigerated air-conditioning is not necessary. Above, pool outside master bedroom.

Though situated irregularly, the concrete columns are placed carefully to shape the flowing interior space where floor, wall, and ceiling blend.

Above left, copper-sheathed fireplace. The house follows the sloping topography of the site by incorporating several stairs and terraces.

Below left and right, workspace furniture is designed to match the house's architecture in the same way that the Prairie house architects often designed furnishings that organically flowed from the design of the architecture. At the end of day, the blue light of the desert dusk fills the house through the many clerestory windows.

Left and right, while the ground level echoes the irregularities and the stony textures of the desert floor, which includes native boulders, the structure and ceiling canopies use modern manufactured materials. Though the space seems complex, it is essentially a single space with different functions for conversation, cooking, sleeping and working articulated as specific spaces carved out of the whole.

Pages 264–65, a designed waterfall emerges from the natural rock and Kellogg's complementary concrete shapes.

Above, decorative elements, such as doors and fixtures, were designed and fabricated by builder John Vugrin. Right, the master suite is at the house's highest point. Though private, it looks down the spine of the house to the main spaces. Views of the desert can be seen through the clerestory windows between the roof canopies.

Left, master bathroom. Sinks and fixtures were custom designed to blend with the organic shapes of the boulders and the house.

Below, view of pool off master bedroom.

Right, bathroom sink.

Pages 270–71, though made of concrete, the house sits lightly on its site. Organic architects have explored the full potential of the material by creating habitations in difficult locations.

ACKNOWLEDGMENTS

In the beginning, Modern architecture had been about the endless possibilities that new technology would allow architects to imagine and build. Organic architects never forgot that.

I first encountered Organic architecture from my grandmother, a faithful reader of *House Beautiful* magazine. Under editor Elizabeth Gordon in the 1950s, it became the virtual house organ for Frank Lloyd Wright's Taliesin Fellowship. But later, in architecture school at UCLA, I learned that there was more to Organic design than Wright's serene, idealized forms based on natural principles. When John Beach, one of my professors, first showed architect Bruce Goff's work to our class just a few weeks into our first year, he revealed an unimagined and subversive universe of form, color, and space that started with Wright and then ventured far beyond. Along with a few other Organic architects, Goff staked out the farthest outposts of Modern design. The daring, the shocking otherliness of Goff's architecture (the young Frank Gehry thought of him as "a shadowy mystical figure") had shunted him out of the architectural mainstream, but had not stopped him from building.

The cultural chasm between establishment Modernism (the mechanistic, flat-roofed boxes that grew out of the Bauhaus) and Organic Modernism was fully on display when Goff came to speak at UCLA in the spring of 1978. He attracted an atypical crowd for architecture lectures. One group of community college students arrived by bus from an architecture program in the hinterlands. The group seemed awestruck by the presence of Goff in his gold lamé jacket, chartreuse shirt, and turquoise bolo tie. A crank in the audience made a rambling statement about transcendence and ecology, concluding by declaring Goff the King of Architecture. Goff shrugged; after fifty years in architecture, he was used to eccentricity—he literally operated from a different center than the customary.

But it became clear to me that Organic architecture, no matter how profoundly unconventional, was emphatically architectural. On a cross-country road trip after graduation, I visited several Goff houses in Oklahoma and met several of his clients. I saw for myself that they were no more the oddballs and fringe misfits imagined by the architecture establishment than was Goff himself. They were solid Middle Americans with a passionate appreciation for creative spaces, practical invention, and modern life. This should not be a surprise to anyone familiar with twentieth-century design; the same region and people had invented and nurtured the Prairie style seventy years before. Goff, the Oklahoma native, tapped these deep springs of culture long after the mainstream had passed them by. So did Lloyd Wright, John Lautner, Fay Jones, Ken Kellogg, Alden Dow, and the other architects presented in this book. They championed the other Modernism.

• • •

We thank the many owners of the houses included in this book for their generosity in allowing us to visit and photograph their homes. They include Peggy Bang, John Bowler, Barbara Brenton, Jacqueline and Phillip Burchill, Chuck Ensminger, Jonathan Formanek, Allen Green, Jill Hillman, Martyl Langsdorf, Dr. and Mrs. Jeffrey Lanier, Maurice and Sue Mazur, Robert McCoy, Ron McKenzie, Rosemary Albo Oxenberg, Rupert Pole, Carol and William Pollak, Joe Price, Brad and June Prince, John Psyllos, Janet Richards, Sidney Robinson, John and Marilyn Roscoe, JoAnn Segel, Mel Shapiro, Joel Silver, Steve Skilken, Jayne Stebbins, Laura and John Warriner, and Don Wetmore.

Our great thanks also go to the architects who continue the Organic tradition today. These include Helena Arahuete, Wallace Cunningham, Ken Kellogg, Mickey Muennig, Alfred Browning Parker, Bart Prince, and Eric Lloyd Wright. Our apologies to the many other architects who we were not able to include here.

Many other people helped with research, aid, and insights. For this, our thanks to Michael Brichford, Ellen Compton and the University of Arkansas Special Collections Archives, Jay and Beverly Doolittle, Ron Drees and the Houston Metropolitan Research Center, Stephen Fox, Jean Kamrath Gonzales, Joel Haertling, Randolph Henning, Mrs. Lu Howe, Maurice Jennings and Davied McKee, Ben Koush, Craig McDonald and the Alden Dow Home and Studio, the Minneapolis Institute of Arts, Jan Novie and Aaron G. Green Associates, and Daniel Roush of Vinci-Hamp Architects. •

BIBLIOGRAPHY

Amin, Kamal. *Reflections from the Shining Brow: My Years with Frank Lloyd Wright and Olgivanna Lazovich.* Santa Barbara, CA: Fithian Press, 2004.

"Architect Lloyd Wright: His Life and Work." *Space Design,* no. 182, November 1979.

Barry, Joseph. *The House Beautiful Treasury of Contemporary American Homes.* New York: Hawthorn Books, Inc., 1958.

Beach, John. "Lloyd Wright's Sowden House." *Fine Homebuilding,* no. 14, April/May 1983.

Blum, Betty J. "Oral History of Robert Paul Schweikher." The Ernest R. Graham Study Center for Architectural Drawings, Department of Architecture, The Art Institute of Chicago, 1984.

Bragdon, Claude Fayette. *The Frozen Fountain: Being Essays on Architecture and the Art of Design in Space.* New York: A. A. Knopf, 1932.

Brooks, H. Allen. *The Prairie School: Frank Lloyd Wright and His Midwest Contemporaries.* New York: W. W. Norton & Co. Inc., 1972.

"Bruce Goff: An Architectural Original." *Inland Architect,* no. 8 (vol. 23), December 1979.

Cheney, Sheldon. *The New World Architecture.* New York: Tudor Publishing Co., 1930.

Cook, Jeffrey. *The Architecture of Bruce Goff.* New York: Harper & Row, Publishers. 1978.

DeLong, David G. *Bruce Goff: Toward Absolute Architecture.* Cambridge, MA: The MIT Press, 1988.

Eaton, Leonard K. *Two Chicago Architects and Their Clients: Frank Lloyd Wright and Howard Van Doren Shaw.* Cambridge, MA: The MIT Press, 1969.

Escher, Frank, ed. *John Lautner, Architect.* London: Artemis, 1994.

Fox, Stephen. *Houston Architectural Guide.* Houston: The American Institute of Architects/Houston Chapter and Herring Press, 1999.

Frampton, Kenneth. *Modern Architecture: A Critical History.* London: Thames and Hudson, 1985.

Friedland, Roger and Harold Zellman. *The Fellowship: The Untold Story of Frank Lloyd Wright & the Taliesin Fellowship.* New York: Regan Books, 2006.

"Friends of Kebyar." *Architecture and Urbanism,* no. 174, March 1985.

Gebhard, David, and Harriette Von Breton. *Lloyd Wright: Architect.* Santa Barbara: The Regents of the University of California, 1971.

Germany, Lisa. *Harwell Hamilton Harris.* Berkeley: University of California Press, 2000.

Guggenheimer, Tobias S. *A Taliesin Legacy: The Architecture of Frank Lloyd Wright's Apprentices.* New York: Van Nostrand Reinhold, 1995.

Hess, Alan, and Alan Weintraub. *The Architecture of John Lautner.* New York: Rizzoli International, 1999.

_____. *Frank Lloyd Wright: The Houses.* New York: Rizzoli International, 2005.

_____. *Hyperwest: American Residential Architecture on the Edge.* London: Thames and Hudson, 1997.

Hochstim, Jan. *Florida Modern: Residential Architecture 1945–1970.* New York: Rizzoli International, 2004.

Ivy, Robert Adams Jr. *Fay Jones.* New York: McGraw-Hill, 1992.

Jones, Fay. *Outside the Pale: The Architecture of Fay Jones.* Fayetteville, Arkansas: University of Arkansas Press, 1999.

Kaufmann, Edgar, and Ben Raeburn, eds. *Frank Lloyd Wright: Writings and Buildings.* Cleveland, OH: The World Publishing Co., 1960.

Langworthy, J. Lamont, with Katherine McNeil. *Hillside Homes: 12 in Laguna Beach, CA.* Santa Rosa, CA: Io Publishing Co., 1982.

McCoy, Esther. "Sim Bruce Richards." *Nature in Architecture* catalog, San Diego Natural History Museum, April–June 1984.

Mead, Christopher Curtis. *The Architecture of Bart Prince: A Pragmatics of Place.* New York: W. W. Norton & Co., Inc. 1999.

Nelson, George, and Henry Wright. *Tomorrow's House.* New York: Simon and Schuster, 1945.

Parker, Alfred Browning. *You and Architecture: A Practical Guide to the Best in Building.* New York: Dial Press, 1965.

Pfeiffer, Bruce Brooks, ed. *Letters to Apprentices: Frank Lloyd Wright.* Fresno, CA: The Press at California State University, Fresno, 1982.

Prince, Bart and David G. DeLong. "Bruce Goff: 1904–1982." *L'Architecture d'Aujourd'hui,* no. 227, June 1983.

Rattenbury, John. *A Living Architecture: Frank Lloyd Wright and Taliesin Architects.* San Francisco: Pomegranate Communications, Inc., 2000.

Robinson, Sidney K. *The Architecture of Alden B. Dow.* Detroit: Wayne State University Press, 1983.

Sergeant, John and Stephen Mooring, eds. "Bruce Goff." *Architectural Design Profiles 16,* no. 10 (vol. 48), 1978.

Stoughton, Kathleen, curator. *Wallace E. Cunningham.* San Diego: Mesa College Art Gallery, 1991.

Sullivan, Louis H. *The Autobiography of an Idea.* New York: Dover Publications, 1956.

Thomas, George E., Michael J. Lewis, and Jeffrey A. Cohen. *Frank Furness: The Complete Works.* New York: Princeton Architectural Press, 1991.

Weintraub, Alan. *Lloyd Wright: The Architecture of Frank Lloyd Wright Jr.* London: Thames & Hudson, 1998.

Young, Lucie. "The Nabobs Love It and Rough It: Mickey Muennig." *New York Times,* May 6, 1987.

"Your Legacy from Frank Lloyd Wright." *House Beautiful,* no. 10 (vol. 101), October 1959.

REFERENCE LIST

Wallace E. Cunningham, Inc.
PO Box 371493
San Diego, CA 92137
619.293.7640
info@wallacecunningham.com

Ken Kellogg
29115-K Valley Center Rd., #109
Valley Center, CA 92082
760.742.1255

Lautner Associates
Helena Arahuete, Architect
8055 W. Manchester Ave., Ste. 705
Playa Del Rey, CA 90293
310.577.7783
www.lautnerassociates.com

Mickey Muennig
PO Box 92
Big Sur, CA 93920
mickey@mickeymuennig.com

Bart Prince, Architect
3501 Monte Vista NE
Albuquerque, NM 87106
505.256.1961
architect@bartprince.com

Eric Lloyd Wright & Associates
Architecture and Planning
24680 Piuma Rd.
Malibu, CA 90265
818.591.8992
studio@elwright.net

INDEX

Aalto, Alvar, 7–8, 76

Adler and Sullivan architectural firm, 12

Arahuete, Helena: as Organic architect, 186, 188; designs Roscoe house, 240–53

Arango house, 79

Armèt and Davis architectural firm, 6, 76

Art Moderne, 15

Arts and Crafts movement, 12, 15

Barnstone, Howard, 80

Barry, Joseph, 78

Bauhaus style: Modernism of, 6, 8, 9, 15, 45; as official architectural school, 41, 186

Bavinger house, 81

Bell house, 79

Bennett house, Edward (Smokey Mountains), 44

Berlage, Hernik, 14, 45

Big Three Industries Building (Houston, Texas), 81

Blythe, James E., 14; home of, 14, 24–29

Bollman house, Henry, 79

Boston Avenue Church, 15

Bowler house (Palos Verde, California), 7, 79, 134–39

Bragdon, Claude: as ornamental designer, 6, 81; admires Sullivan, 45, 76

Brenton house, Stanley (Boulder, Colorado), 81, 156–61

Bugenhagen and Turnbull, 14

Bull, Charles Livingston, 32

Byrnes, Barry: works for Frank Lloyd Wright, 12, 14, 15; design of, 13

Callister, Charles Warren, 76

Case Study houses, 6, 77

Chemosphere house, 188

Cheney, Charles, 45

Cheney, Mamah, 14

Cheney, Sheldon, 40, 45

Chicago: as architectural laboratory, 12

Chicago School, 8, 12, 44

Church of Christ the King (Tulsa, Oklahoma), 15

Concrete, earthen, 7, 13, 25

Concrete block homes, 38

Coonley house, 14

Corbusier, Le, 45

Crescent house (San Diego, California), 4, 228–39

Cunningham, Wallace: designs Crescent house, 4, 228–39; as Organic architect, 186, 188

Dana house, Susan Lawrence, 91

De Klerk, Michel, 7

Desert house (Joshua Tree, California), 188–89, 254–71, 276

Dow, Alden, is inspired by Frank Lloyd Wright, 6, 13, 38, 40, 65; house designs of, 41, 43; designs Hanson house, 64–69; in popular magazines, 77; controversial designs of, 77, 187; influences designs of Midland, Michigan, 80

Dow, Herbert, 41, 42

Drake, Blaine, 76

Drummond, William, 12, 14

Dudok, Willem, 45

Eaton, Leonard, 15

Eckbo, Garrett, 97

Eichler, Joseph, 6, 76

Elin house, 44

Elmslie, George, 12, 14, 15

Elrod house, 79

Elting, Winston, 45

Emerson, Ralph Waldo: inspires Organic architecture, 6, 8–9, 12, 45, 186

Emerson Unitarian Church, 81n

Environmentalism, 81

Fallingwater, 9, 40, 45

Farnsworth house, 45

Field Warehouse, 44

Ford house (Aurora, Illinois), 79, 81, 82–89

Frampton, Kenneth, 76

Frankl, Paul, 41

Friends of Kebyar, 76

Furness, Frank, 6, 8–9

Furness, William Henry, 8–9

Gale house, 13

Garden, Hugh, 12

Gehry, Frank, 8, 186

Goff, Bruce: 87; as Organic architect, 6, 7, 9, 14, 15, 186; is similar to Schweikher, 44; is influenced by Bragdon, 45; following World War II, 76; in popular magazines, 77; promotes teaching of Organic architecture, 78; is ignored by House Beautiful, 78; forms own school of Organic architecture, 78–79, 80, 81, 187; designs Ford house, 82–89; designs Pollock–Warriner house, 108–13

Gordon, Elizabeth, 6–7, 78, 81

Green, Aaron: as Organic architect, 40, 76, 78; joins Taliesin Fellowship, 79; designs Green house, 178–85

Green house, 178–85

Greene, Herb, 78

Griffin, Walter Burley: as Organic architect, 6, 14; works for Frank Lloyd Wright, 12; style of, 12–13; Mason City houses of, 13; designs in Australia, 15; designs Melson house, 20–23; designs Blythe house, 24–29

Gropius, Walter: as architect, 9, 41, 45, 186; leads Harvard School of Design, 77

Guggenheim Museum, 76–77

Gurdjieff, G. I., 40, 45, 186

Haertling, Charles: as Organic architect, 6, 81; designs Willard-Shapiro house, 126–33; designs Brenton house, 156–61;

Hamlin, Talbot, 77

Hanson house (Midland, Michigan), 64–69

Häring, Hugo, 7

Harris, Harwell Hamilton, 78, 80

Hearst retreat, William Randolph (San Simeon, California), 45

Heller house, 13

Henken, David, 76

Heurtley house, 13

Hight house, 189

Hill, John deKoven, 78

Hillmer, Jack, 76

Hollyhock house, 38

House Beautiful, 77, 78, 81

Howe, John, 77

Hubbard, Elbert, 12

Hunt, Myron, 12

Imperial Hotel (Tokyo, Japan), 6, 15, 44

International Style, 6, 8. 9, 40, 41, 78

Jacobs house, 40

Jencks, Charles, 186

Jester, Ralph, 81

Johnson, Herbert, 40

Johnson, Paul, 78

Johnson, Philip, 80

Johnson Wax Building, 6, 40

Jones, A. Quincy, 79

Jones, Fay: is inspired by Frank Lloyd Wright, 6, 76; in popular magazines, 77, 78; on Goff and his architectural department, 79; is part of Taliesin Fellowship, 80; designs Pine Knoll, 140–49; designs Stoneflower, 150–55; architectural style of, 187

Kamrath, Karl, 80

Kamrath house, Karl (Houston, Texas), 96–101

Kaufmann, Edgar, 40

Keck, George Fred, 9

Keller house, K. T., 43

Kellogg, Ken: as Organic architect, 186, 188–89; designs Desert house, 188–89, 254–71, 276

Kelsey, Albert, 6

Klutho, Henry, 8, 14

Knitlock system, 13

Koolhaas, Rem, 8, 186

Kramer, Piet, 7

Lautner, John: as Organic architect, 6, 40; uses earthen concrete, 7, 13, 14; following World War II, 76; is ignored by House Beautiful, 78; pushes boundaries of Organic architecture, 79, 81, 187–88; designs Silvertop house, 114–21; designs Segel house, 168–77

Lewis house, Herbert (Park Ridge, Illinois), 44

Ligar, George Frank, 76

MacKie, Fred, 80

MacKie and Kamrath architectural firm, 76, 80

Madison Unitarian Church (Madison, Wisconsin), 43

Maher, George, 12, 15

Mahoney, Marion, 12, 14

Malin, Leonard, 188

Marin County Civic Center, 76–77, 80

Martin house, Darwin, 91

Mason City, Iowa, 14

Mayne, Thom, 186

McCoy, Esther, 76, 80

Melson house, J. G. (Mason City, Iowa), 12, 14, 20–23

Mendelsohn, Eric, 45

Mendocino County house, 188

Mid-Century Modern, 6, 7, 76

Midland Country Club (Midland, Michigan), 41

Mies van der Rohe, Ludwig: as architect, 9, 41; as director of School of Architecture, 77, 79

Mile-High Skyscraper, 76

Mills, Mark, 76

Modernism, 12, 77

Morris, William, 12

Mosher, Bob, 40

Mossberg house (South Bend, Indiana), 90–95

Muennig, Mickey: as Organic architect, 6, 78, 186, 187; designs Partington Ridge House II, 190–205

MVRDV, 186

Neckendorn, Antonin, 14

Nelson, George, 81n

Niemeyer, Oscar, 8, 13, 76, 77

Organic architecture: development of, 6–7, 12–15; key architects of, 7–8; reemergence of, 45; after World War II, 76–80; current practice of, 186–89

Oud, J. J. P., 45

Ouspensky, Peter D., 45

Pacific Coast house, 77, 79

Page house, Harry (Mason City, Iowa), 13

Pann's (Los Angeles, California), 6

Paris Exposition of 1926, 9, 15

Parker, Alfred Browning: as Organic architect, 76, 78, 80–81; designs Woodsong house, 162–67

Partington Ridge House II (Big Sur, California), 190–205

Paul house (Aspen, Colorado), 78

Pei, I. M., 78

Perkins, Dwight, 12

Peters, William Wesley, 40

Píetila, Reima, 7–8

Pine Knoll house (Little Rock, Arkansas), 80, 140–49

Pole house (Los Angeles, California), 122–25

Pollock–Warriner house (Oklahoma City, Oklahoma), 79, 108–13

Post Modernism, 76

Post Ranch Inn, 188

Prairie style, 8, 12–15, 189n

Price, Joe, 79

Price house (Corona del Mar, California), 189

Price Tower (Bartlesville, Oklahoma), 6

Prince, Bart: designs Sun Valley house, 2, 206–17; as Organic architect, 78, 186, 188; designs Prince home and Hight house, 189; designs Skilken house, 218–27

Prince home, Brad and June, 189

Psyllos house (Big Sur, California), 187

Purcell, William Gray, 12, 14, 15

Purcell and Elmslie: design Purcell-Cutts house, 10–11, 30–37; as Prairie-style architects, 14, 15

Purcell-Cutts house, William and Edna (Minneapolis, Minnesota): views of, 10–11, 30–37; Prairie-style of, 14, 66

Rand, Ayn, 41, 188

Rant house, 44

Rebhuhn house, Ben, 79

Richards, Sim Bruce, 40, 76; in Taliesin Fellowship, 80; own home and studio, 102–7

Richards house, Sim Bruce (San Diego, California), 102–7

Richardson, Henry Hobson, 8, 44

Roberts house, Isabel (River Forest, Illinois), 16–19

Robie house, 13

Rock Crest–Rock Glen development (Mason City, Iowa), 14

Rogers, James Gamble, 12

Roosevelt, Theodore Jr., home of, 9

Roscoe house (Vacaville, California), 188, 240–53

Rosenbaum house, Stanley and Mildred, 79

Rudolph, Paul, 78

Rule house, Arthur (Mason City, Iowa), 13

Saarinen, Eero, 76

Saarinen, Eliel, 41, 45

Samuel-Navarro house (Los Angeles, California), 38, 39

Savoie, Villa, 45

Scargle house, W. Russell (Glenview, Illinois), 44

Scharoun, Hans, 76

Schindler, R. M., 9, 15, 45

Schmidt, Richard, 12

Schneider house, Samuel (Mason City, Iowa), 13

Schweikher, Paul: has new vision of architecture, 6, 43–45, 76; home of, 44, 70–75

Sea Ranch Chapel (Sea Ranch, California), 6

Segel house (Malibu, California), 79, 81, 168–77

Shaw, Howard Van Doren, 12

Silsbee, J. L., 14

Silvertop house (Los Angeles, California), 79, 114–21

Skilken house (Columbus, Ohio), 218–27

Smith, Pamela, 231

Soleri, Paolo, 76

Sowden house, John and Ruth (Los Angeles, California), 38, 79, 54–63

Spencer, Robert, 12

Stevens house (Malibu, California), 77, 81

Stevenson house (Fort Worth, Texas), 81n

Stoneflower house (Eden Isle, Arkansas), 80, 150–55

Storer house (Los Angeles, California), 46–53

Sturges house, 97

Sullivan, Louis: architectural start of, 6; death of, 6, 45; as Organic architect, 7–9, 12, 186; firm of, 14

Sultanyan, George, 231

Sun Valley house (Sun Valley, Idaho), 2, 206–17

Tafel, Edgar, 40, 76

Taggart house, 38, 79, 42

Taliesin Fellowship: keeps Organic architecture alive, 9; is established by Frank Lloyd Wright, 40–41, 43–44; young architects of, 79–80; organization of, 186–87

Textile-block system, 13, 38, 47

Thomas, George, 8

Trost, Henry C., 8, 14

Turner house (Aspen, Colorado), 77

Unity Temple, 12

Upton house (Paradise Valley, Arizona), 44–45

Urban, Joseph, 41

Usonian Automatic houses: Frank Lloyd Wright designs, 40, 44, 71; cooperative for, 45; are overseen by Howe, 77; Taliesin apprentices work on, 80

Van der Vlugt, L. C., 45

Vugrin, John, 266

Walker house (Carmel, California), 77

Walter house (Iowa), 77

Wasmuth portfolio drawings, 13, 38

Wayfarer's Chapel (Palos Verdes, California), 76

West, Guy, 231

Whitman, Walt, 8, 186

Willard-Shapiro house (Boulder, Colorado), 81, 126–33

Wisconsin State Capitol, 78

Wolfe and Wolfe, 8, 14

Wood butchers, 81

Woodsong house (Coconut Grove, Florida), 162–67

Wright, Eric Lloyd: adds pool to Storer house, 48; as Organic architect, 80; designs Pole house, 122–25

Wright, Frank Lloyd: inspires new architects, 6, 41–42, 44–45, 79; as Organic architect, 6–8, 12, 13, 14–15, 186; develops textile-block system, 13; on Organic architecture, 13; designs Roberts house, Isabel, 16–19; returns to Organic designs, 38; establishes Taliesin Fellowship, 40–41, 43, 186–87; designs Storer house, 46–53; following World War II, 76; designs Walter house, 77; is in popular magazines, 77; promotes himself, 78; designs Mossberg house, 90–95

Wright, Henry, 81n

Wright, Lloyd: designs Bowler house, 7; keeps Organic architecture alive, 9, 15, 38; develops textile-block system, 13; designs own house and studio, 38, 40–41; designs Sowden house, 38, 54–63; designs Samuel-Navarro house, 38–39; designs Taggart house, 38, 42

Wright, Olgivanna, 40, 186–87

Wurster, William, 9